DREAM

ANOTHER DREAM

T0204818

CHOOSE YOUR FUTURE, **CONQUER** YOUR PAST,

LEAD WITH CONFIDENCE

TYSON D. THOMPSON

TYSON D. THOMPSON

DREAM ANOTHER DREAM

Published By: Courageous Publishing

Edited By: Terralyn Roach, TSR Creative, Louisville, Kentucky

Copy Edited By: Brooklyn Russell,
B. Russ Innovations, Merrillville, Indiana.

Cover Design: Tyson D. Thompson, Tulsa, Oklahoma

Photo By: Monica Burgess Photography, Tulsa, Oklahoma

Scriptures Quotes: King James, Amplified,
and New International versions of the Bible.

ISBN: 978-1-7360204-0-1

Dedication

to

The Matriarch, My Muse

I feel it's very appropriate and important to give honor where honor is due. It would be remiss of me not to speak of the woman who exemplified everything she taught me. My mother's story is significant to my personal story as the many lessons I learned from her helped me to navigate, strategize, and thrive.

After being rejected by her father—physically and verbally, abused by her first and second husbands, suffering the tragic death of her one-year-old child and only daughter, losing her mother to cancer, and battling and defeating cancer herself after refusing radiation treatment, my mother still managed to send me out into the world convinced that life was worth living, and I had the power to live it well. Her greatest desire was for my brothers and me to have a good quality of life. But her philosophy was centered around the idea that PEOPLE are what's most valuable, and we should help them regardless of our circumstances.

There were times when it seemed as though all hell broke loose in our lives as a family. But my mother had an uncanny ability to remain calm and faithful to her principles. Even during our darkest hours, her lessons—which were rarely about money or material things—always led us back to the light. And that light took us on paths that revealed valuable lessons that were instrumental in the development of our character.

I don't believe my mother ever realized that the principles and life lessons she taught would be my inheritance. They are what I've chosen to live by, as they have been foundational in my ability to enjoy a beautiful and fulfilling life. I'm not suggesting that it's always without trauma or stress-free. Still, it's a life filled with hope and aspirations to conquer difficulties regardless of how overwhelming they may be.

My mother's guidance may not have always been perfect. But I believe in her efforts to prepare me to be the kind of man that is well-equipped to overcome adversity. Her real-life voice of reason has become my legacy that I now want to share with others.

TYSON D. THOMPSON

Contents

TYSON D. THOMPSON

FOREWORD

DREAM ANOTHER DREAM is the unvarnished voice of a barber known throughout Tulsa, Oklahoma, as "Tyson." I know him as the man with words of confidence and hope, which he shares with each person who's fortunate enough to have him as their barber. I've been one of those people for years.

As a published author myself, I'm often asked questions about how to become a successful writer. However, the questions are usually ones I'm unable to answer. But one day, this Tulsa barber extraordinaire asked, "Mr. Taulbert, I know you don't have the time, but would you consider reading a manuscript I've been working on for some time now?"

I really wanted to decline his request, but he had the clippers in his hand, working on my hair. I didn't want the clippers to slip. With a little reservation, I said, "I will when I get some time."

I was completely unsure of what his book would be about. I knew nothing about cutting hair, but I did know that he had taken his barbershop beyond the ordinary to a high level of excellence. It was indeed the place to see and be seen—where men and women of diverse races came to get the "Tyson" touch. Therefore, I was prepared to get a lesson in "Barbering 101" when I read his manuscript.

Tyson e-mailed his manuscript to me, but it waited patiently for me in my inbox for days and weeks. Finally, I opened it and began reading, but I had no idea where it would take me and what I would discover along the way. It revealed an unexpected personal journey through the turbulent waters of his life. I was captivated by his family history, which many of us would find too difficult to share.

DREAM ANOTHER DREAM takes you through turbulent waters and rays of hope—one man's journey that continues to unfold. Tyson, the Barber of Tulsa, takes his readers to places they've never been or have sworn never to go again. He gives conversations from the heart where the soul of the language fills you both with night-fear and an insatiable appetite for rays of hope. Readers will experience the heart and the soul of this writer—a young black man— who, while growing up, had every reason in the world never to dream and navigate beyond the "hood" that sought to hold him captive.

While reading Tyson's story, my face burned with hot tears as I cried for him, and along with him. The pages are filled with a reality no child should have witnessed or be forced to remember. The strength and resolve of his mother leap off the pages, assuring me that the sun would shine again. Tyson's story captures more than his personal journey. It also captures the heartaches of others who never share aloud and the dreams of so many that became raisins in the sun.

DREAM ANOTHER DREAM is a story of a place where both failure and success fought to own the turf of Tyson's soul. He is a man who yells loudly to those who are often overlooked and believe they have no choices.

Tyson is an artist who has taken the broken pieces of his life and created an altar to which others can come and listen to the oracle of HIS truth. In so doing, they will find their way to *DREAM ANOTHER DREAM.*

— Clifton LeMoure Taulbert, *Prize-Winning Author*

"Once Upon a Time When We Were Colored"
"The Last Train North"
"Eight Habits of the Heart"
"The Invitation"

INTRODUCTION

I f you're anything like me, the monotony of figuring out LIFE as you live can become a nagging thorn that pricks at your morale. And if we're not careful, we run the risk of viewing life and the people we love from a cynical and condescending perspective. Therefore, we stop listening, leaving a lot of people living much of their lives unheard. Not listening also causes them to disconnect with their inner voice and the ability to hear others' concerns. They become deaf-mutes, unknowingly leaving a trail of lifeless relationships and suppressed dreams. I know this to be true because I lived this way for many years. However, I have since chosen an alternative outlook. I can now assure you that life is good, and dreams can be your reality. But it started with me understanding my VALUE.

As a professional master barber, I've been privileged to occupy a front-row seat to the lives of countless individuals for more than thirty years now. During this time, I've observed and studied their behaviors, attitudes, and beliefs that have consistently resulted in their greatest successes and their most demoralizing failures.

After more than one hundred thousand, one-on-one conversations with patrons from all over the world, I see that many variables hinder us from overcoming the ordinary trials of life. But there is a crucial component for living successfully through conflict that I've found to be universally lacking with most individuals, including myself. We fail to experience the best life has to offer because we unconsciously overlook what is authentically valuable in every moment: EACH OTHER.

It is normal to feel overwhelmed with life, especially after experiencing traumatic events. Memories of such times have a way of invading and consuming our thoughts, even long after the events have ended. These bad memories can cause us to destroy the very relationships meant to facilitate our growth so we can move forward in fulfilling our purpose despite our past. And if we allow ourselves to become disengaged in our relationships, our responsiveness to what matters most is almost non-existent.

We can eradicate any disdain we've had for our painful tragedies by heeding every moment that commands our undivided attention from this moment forward. Life is always speaking to us, but we must always listen. To do so, we must be willing to let go of all cynicism birthed from our mayhem and give up our right to persist in anger.

I'll be the first to admit that this life is not what I thought it would be. It's as if life is at odds with itself, appearing to be somewhat contradictory at best, perhaps even a little bipolar. At this very moment, someone is celebrating the birth of a child, but tomorrow may have to lay a loved one who was tragically murdered to rest. Time and time again, proving to be extraordinarily volatile and unfair, life sure had me fooled. To sum it up, I often thought life sucked.

In my innocence, I had unrealistic ideas about dreams. I thought my desires were guaranteed to become a reality and would be free of opposition if I'd just set some goals and do my best to achieve them. I also foolishly figured if I would just treat people with respect, they'd willingly reciprocate the same respect and kindness. I also believed the idea that parents always do what's best for their children. But as life tested my resolve, I eventually discovered that life is habitually unpredictable. Furthermore, living the "good life" is not a turnkey experience- nothing happens automatically. Some things are ideal, but it takes more than dreaming for them to become real.

The narrative of my life reads like an emotional war novel. My story reveals a long list of failed battles and destructive beliefs, which ultimately discharged me from the fight to live my dreams. A trail of fragments composed of oppressive shrapnel lodged itself deep into my soul only to paralyze me, thus, hindering me from developing healthy relationships. The perpetual chaos eventually prompted me to ask myself this question: "Is conflict the only plot for my human experience?"

After years of probing for an answer, I concluded that the answer to my question might be "yes." And quite frankly, I find it impressive that—as a human being—I'm able to survive in a system such as this. What's even more impressive is the fact that I'm not alone. The truth is that we're all perfectly human and humanly flawed, which qualifies us as a little foolish at times.

Life comes with its share of troubles–some we initiate, and some of no fault of our own. However, we must recognize and acknowledge any part we've played in our struggles and take full responsibility for our undesirable circumstances. It's often just a series of poor decisions that derail us from the tracks meant to carry us to successful relationships and careers. Some of us have squandered money like drug addicts. Many people have lied to get their way and cheated to get ahead. While others stole to get what they wanted quicker, they anxiously pursued the wrong mate, while pridefully pointing their fingers at others for their downfalls. Yes, we sometimes allow our pain to create pain for others. But don't fret; there's hope for redemption.

With my story, I want to share how anyone can change their life narrative and thrive beyond past disappointments. Trust me; it is possible to recapture your inner voice, restore your confidence, and enjoy an incredible life without being hindered by the lingering regrets of your past. You will soon learn how to use those regrets as catapults to propel you towards a better way of living. I'm not suggesting that you will never again encounter more situations that can be potentially devastating The difference is that you won't have to fear them. The choice to win in this life is and always has been yours. You can transform disheartening situations into milestones as every challenge creates new opportunities to develop your character and become the best version of yourself. The difficulty is for prompting you to *EMBRACE YOUR INNATE VALUE AS A HUMAN BEING.*

By the time you finish reading this book, you will be inspired and empowered to tackle new dreams and discover a whole new world, free of the fear of rejection and defeat. You will become more optimistic in this capricious time and space we call "life." Though probably, neither your circumstances nor anyone around you will ever change, YOU WILL. That makes what others do or choose not to do irrelevant. Understand that it's YOUR perspective and how YOU respond to situations that give you power. You were born equipped to overcome hardship. We all were. Think about this fact. Despite the many historical disasters that have taken place since the beginning of time, humanity continues to thrive. Your problems are not the end of you. They often help you to FIND YOU.

Using stories from my early years as a child, followed by my most recent years as an adult, I outlined the values for anyone to thrive. Discover how to restore relationships, build confidence through effective communication, and *DREAM ANOTHER DREAM* when an original dream didn't work. You will discover the principles I studied from my dearly beloved mother and the concepts I learned from my thirty years as a business owner and mentor. Why is this important? So, you can live free to focus on what matters most: PEOPLE. You will also be able to pursue the dreams in your heart that you were born to achieve. Let's get this journey started.

CHAPTER ONE:
SECURED: THE DREAMERS VALUE

"You did not choose me, but I chose you
and appointed you so that you might go
and bear fruit…"

— John 15:16 (New International Version)

We had nothing at all to do with our existence. We didn't choose this life; it seems to have chosen us when we consider the fact that there's nothing of our existence we controlled. Our families, appearance, culture, nationality, ethnicity, personality, temperament, and predisposition were all dealt with without our permission. But this can appear unfair when you consider how many of us were born during hostile times, suffer from physical or mental disabilities, inherited abusive parents, or born in adverse poverty. Yet, we have remained resilient in our efforts to preserve the only existence we know. And despite life's never-ending conflicts, we have been chosen. The last time I checked, anything chosen has a purpose, and with purpose comes VALUE.

From the beginning of time, LIFE has been the common thread that unites all people groups despite our differences. Hence, regardless of what we believe, whether in reincarnation, evolution, or creation by an intentional God, we can agree that we, as human beings, do not exist of our merit. Furthermore, on our birthdays, life said yes from the time when something or someone beyond our influence gave us consciousness.

One definition of life is "The existence of organic matter, including the capacity for growth, reproduction, purposeful activity, and continual change preceding death." In essence, life was given with requirements— our growth, development, productivity, and the flexibility for change until our last breath.

So, what are you doing with your life that helps you grow, develop, and be productive? If you can't clearly define it, perhaps you're not as aware of your value and your DREAMS' significance, as you may think. Even if you're a victim of unfavorable circumstances, you matter, and so does your story. Why? Because inherently, you are valuable— LIFE chose you.

I don't know absolutely what each person is purposed to do, but this I know, to thrive in this life, we have to be intentional. Anything truly alive will GROW, DEVELOP, PRODUCE, and make the necessary CHANGES to become more to add value to the world. I see your worth. Do you? If you haven't already, I challenge you to embrace your value and seize the only moment you currently have— this life.

When our bodies are absent from this life, we are disqualified from participating in the only reality we absolutely know. As for any belief of existence outside of what we tangibly see, we must rely on our faith in something more— settling that our lives and life itself are priceless and unmerited. And by this principle, we can endorse our inherent human value.

Typically, one would say a person's "value" is based on their age, assets, abilities, associations, accolades, accounts, and other assessments. And without a doubt, we are all guilty of sizing individuals up within the first thirty seconds of meeting them. That means we erroneously place value on the superficial instead of the actual person.

We often don't realize how valuable people are until we're done comparing ourselves with them. *Having prestige, prosperity, and popularity usually takes precedence over having meaningful relationships as society teaches us to focus on having "fans" instead of being "friends."* And by the time we become aware of this mistake, we will have passed on or lost interest in developing any kind of relationship we sought to have with them. What mattered is lost.

For years I struggled to connect the dots. I wrestled with my significance because I was supposedly poor and uneducated. Professionally, I viewed myself as an ordinary service provider with limited influence. Though I had achieved some success, I was often riddled with doubt and confused about my identity. Sadly, I shut the world out— becoming intimately crippled. Fearful that people would uncover my vulnerability, I kept my distance. I was selfishly neglecting my relationships to protect my pride. Afraid of rejection, I unconsciously resisted all relationships of value.

Being conscious of our inherent human value is of utmost importance because it demands our devotion towards one another. By default, the life we steward validates us. However, being mindful of each other's worth is an added affirmation of our significance. By deciding to identify with this perspective, the fear of rejection can become non-existent. Like many others, I fought for years to pursue my dreams because I chose to listen to critics (me being the worst of them). But when I discovered how my worth was secure, I was liberated to recapture my inner voice, improve my relationships, restore confidence when lost, and pursue my desires without regrets. You, too, can be empowered to humbly embrace who you are and enjoy the single most important gift we all cherish— the gift of LIFE.

I know you have big dreams, and you will face many opposing forces, such as a lack of resources, fear, discouraging people, laziness, and possibly physical challenges. But when they come, you can be prepared. So, when the haters start talking, and doubt tries to grip you, these are a few questions to help stir up the belief that you matter regardless of your past, your current circumstances, or others' opinions.

1) Did you decide to be born? If your answer is possibly no, then who or what chose you?

And most likely, all people groups exist as a result of the same process. Therefore, we are equal in value, and no one can take it, because they didn't give it. Meaning, that cruel boss or dominating spouse, or any other person that has attempted to lord over you, is no better than you. Think About it.

2) Is it possible that your physical body, job title, income, how you feel, or what others think about you can change? If so, isn't it risky to measure your worth against what can be different tomorrow or change today? Yet, if you decide to believe that your value is inherent, it can never change.

3) Do you talk to yourself? If not, you should. I am my greatest cheerleader. Why? Because I'm always with me. Words of affirmation build faith. That's why I speak to myself when I'm down. I sing uplifting songs when I'm doubtful. Then I go share my story to inspire others— recharging my faith that I'm valuable.

4) Can you grasp the idea that your existence is intentional? If so, these are the benefits of knowing you have been selected:

- Instant validation

- Freedom to pursue dreams

- Courage to conquer your fears

- The belief that you have a purpose and a future.

TYSON D. THOMPSON

CHAPTER TWO:
FREE TO DREAM:
FORGIVENESS

"Freedom is never voluntarily given by the oppressor;
it must be demanded by the oppressed."
— Martin Luther King Jr.

I t was in 1979 while living in Oklahoma City when I witnessed my father dragging my mother out of a small apartment building onto a concrete slab. Daddy was six feet tall and weighed approximately two-hundred twenty pounds. On the other hand, my mother was only five feet and three inches tall and weighed one hundred and twenty pounds. The altercation happened after he had beaten her profusely inside the apartment. My three brothers and I were there together, watching this nightmare unfold. I was only five years old.

Two of my brothers and I ran out of the apartment together. I could barely see because my eyes were burning as tears flooded them and rushed down my face. After wiping my eyes, I soon noticed a small group of people standing out there yelling and screaming. I was confused that no one in the crowd of adults did anything to intervene as my father was manhandling my mother. I thought about speaking up and trying to stop him myself, but I was gripped with fear and very confused. I was so young and very much unprepared for all that was going on. I was overwhelmed with emotion at the sight of my father, who I loved, beating my mother, who I cherished. They were both my heroes, and I couldn't make heads or tails of what I was witnessing.

While the crowd's constant yelling overpowered the atmosphere, my mother's cry demanded my attention. Over the madness, I heard her scream, "Get my kids away! Please don't let them see this!" But as she pleaded to the bystanders, my father began kicking her repeatedly, showing his agitation with her demands. But that didn't stop her from crying out repeatedly, "Please get my kids away!" My father kneeled, grabbed her head, and slammed it several times on the concrete slab. The sound of a human skull repeatedly slammed against concrete was horrific, but my father didn't stop. He was seemingly in a rage beyond his control. But in the midst of it all, my mother remained fixated on my brothers and me. She wanted us removed from the situation, as her plea for someone to take us away was relentless.

The emotions I felt as a five-year-old boy are just as real today whenever I let my mind wander to my father's images beating my mother. The sound of her head being slammed to the ground still echoes in my head. The man I honored because he was my father beat my mother, who was very dear to my heart.

As some of the witnesses finally pulled my brothers and me away from the scene, I looked back at my mother and couldn't help but see the hurt and pain in her eyes. However, when I looked deeper, I was able to see beyond her pain as her soul revealed the unconditional love she had for me. While being assaulted and publicly humiliated, she wanted me to know that she saw my value. It was as if time suddenly stood still.

With disregard for her safety, my mother was more concerned about her sons' wellbeing. I later learned that her reason for trying to get my brothers and me to safety was to escape knowing for sure that we were clear of my father's reach. She instinctively knew that saving us from physical harm would possibly redirect any emotional scars my brothers and I could have potentially developed. She didn't want this event to negatively alter our perspective of life for the rest of our lives.

When my mother realized we were safe, she somehow broke free of my father and ran. Battered and brushed, she frantically knocked on several apartment doors until someone let her in. Once inside, she called the police. It wasn't until several years later that she said anything else about that incident.

Endeavoring to remain positive about her life, she persisted in being steadfast in her belief to never speak negatively of my father or the many witnesses who stood by and did nothing to help her. I will always remember her example of forgiveness. To be beaten and humiliated in front of her children, family, and peers, and still can forgive her abuser, is supernatural. I'm convinced this was the prelude to the many lessons that would eventually shape my amazing life's journey, but it began with an agreement I made to myself.

I declared never to allow that traumatic event to influence me negatively. Instead of becoming a victim of domestic violence, I chose never to harbor anger towards my father. I professed to live my life from an entirely different perspective than his by honoring and respecting people. I also chose never to treat a woman the way he handled my mother. Today, I still find it unthinkable to ball my fist with the intent to punch a lady. I knew my legacy would be different by committing to these choices I made despite what I experienced. It wasn't an easy task, but I was able to see my father's value after sorting through the madness. And because this was my first significant life conflict, accepting his value was a crucial lesson for me to lay the right foundation for my future.

Over the years, I continued valuing my father as my mother led the way by allowing him to remain in my life. Though at times, she shared the truth about his addictions and abusive behavior, the picture she painted of him concealed the rage as she chose to display his better qualities. Her graceful attitude made the process easier. She never slandered his name. However, she made sure that we understood why their relationship had to end.

The real lesson came when my mother established that my father was still necessary. She believed that his position as my father was reason enough for him to remain in my life. She wanted me to honor him by preserving whatever I could of the relationship. So, appreciating my dad's humanity freed me to forgive him and move on with my life. As a result, I was able to honor my father and yet live free from his rejection.

I know you may be thinking that this valuing and forgiving concept sounds good in theory. But I assure you, it is a lifesaver. I know firsthand because years later, my father put me to the test again.

My father wasn't all bad. I do recall an occasional kiss on the cheek as his sandpaper-like mustache pricked my face, saying, "I love you." But those moments were overshadowed by his addictions. The majority of the time, he was under the influence of alcohol or some type of street drug. Therefore, he struggled to have what I considered to be healthy relationships.

I have no recollection of him ever calling me by my name. The only word I recall him using to reference me was when he said (excuse my French), "Shut the fuck up, nigga!" A slap to my face followed this as we entered a local carnival. I was only ten years old and was very embarrassed. It felt as though he stripped me of all my dignity in front of hundreds of people and showed no regard for my feelings. Afterward, he didn't speak to me for the rest of the day. He did this because I pointed out that he may have forgotten to pay for my ticket to enter.

When we arrived back at my mother's home, I told her I would not revisit my father. I was done! But as usual, her words were comforting to me. She sat my brothers and me down to have one of our group discussions. In her very calm and peaceful voice, my mother said:

> *Boys, I don't speak much about your father's negative behaviors. And I'm sorry this happened. I knew one day you'd grow up and see for yourselves how he can be. Now that you've seen it, I want you to understand that his life was not the easiest. His father was a tough man, and his mom didn't always make the best decisions. Alcohol and drugs were prevalent in his life. He never developed in the way he should have. Even though this has happened, he's still your father, but I will not force you to go there.*

At that very moment, I was empowered to drop my offense. It was like déjà vu. ***Again, I forgave Daddy and chose to learn from his mistakes rather than become a victim of his actions.***

Trust me; I know this is a hard act to follow– forgiving someone who seemingly disregards your worth. However, to be free to DREAM, you can't risk internalizing the bad things you've suffered. You may be thinking, Why me? How could they do this to me? I did nothing to deserve this. I don't understand. It's not fair.

No, you probably didn't deserve it. And yes, it was most likely unfair. But being consumed with what's been done to you will paralyze you. Your ability to move forward will be inhibited—not by your abuser—but by your captive thoughts and emotions. Instead of taking it personally, consider the source. Consider what they inflicted on you had more to do with the person they are than you. So, dwelling on it is just a waste of precious time.

Forgiving my father and choosing not to take his actions personally was a powerful move for me. I did it by separating myself from the situation and acknowledging that it was HIS CHOICE to abandon his role as a father, not mine. I viewed HIM as the victim, not me. He lived through many life-scarring events as a kid. Sadly, his response was different than mine. He turned to drugs and other dysfunctional behaviors. My mother helped me understand this about my father and wanted me to take a different path and not perpetuate what would have possibly been a cycle for me and future generations.

My mother never tried to present the reasons for my father's actions as excuses; neither did she want me to use his actions towards me as my excuse. So, I focused on demonstrating that life extends far beyond any traumatic moment I may have experienced.

> *To the executors of my pain, I gave no emotional jurisdiction over my soul. If I had remained offended due to what my father and others did or said to me, I would have given into the worst of humanity. I would have forfeited my opportunity to impact the host of people waiting beyond the walls of my pain to share my best self. I refuse to have a crippling mindset that destroys my connection with people.*

You have the power to forgive, but you must be willing to release what you are inclined to hold close and dear: your pain. Relishing in your pain and making it the backdrop for everything you can't or won't do will only block you. Understand that your offenders can move on to be influential individuals if they forgive themselves and choose a better path while you remain stuck in the same place. The only person your unforgiveness hurts is you. The benefits of forgiveness happen when you value others and your future enough to let go of what happened to you in exchange for all that's in store.

If you're ready to live free from rejection by forgiving the contributors of your pain—including yourself—consider applying the following. It won't be easy, but it's necessary for inner healing, restoring confidence to choose your future and for DREAMING NEW DREAMS.

1) Forgiveness is a choice motivated by the human heart. And it's more than merely saying that you forgive someone. You must make a conscious decision to release all feelings of offense and move forward. Letting go is both an emotional and a physical process. But you can do it.

2) It's possible to *uphold an individual's value and distance yourself emotionally from their negative behavior.* However, there are some extreme cases. If you find yourself in danger get help if needed. By no means should anyone tolerate abuse.

3) Resist personalizing rejection. Everyone has a choice. And if someone chooses to lie on

you, cheat on you, steal from you, or talk down to you, remember, people's treatment of you is not always a reflection of your value.

4) Expecting certain benefits from a relationship when the other person is unwilling or unable to deliver is a waste of time.

5) After assessing your relationships, acknowledge how much influence over your life you have given to someone. Then take it back by respecting yourself. Your thoughts have more impact on your life than other people's opinions of you.

TYSON D. THOMPSON

CHAPTER THREE:
THE POWER OF ANOTHER DREAM

"You are never too old to set another goal or to dream a new dream."

— C. S. Lewis

After my parents divorced, it wasn't long before I found myself in the back seat of an old green station wagon, which seemed to contain everything we owned. My mother, my three brothers, and I were riding up Highway 44 from Oklahoma City, Oklahoma to Tulsa, Oklahoma. At five years old, sitting in the third row of the overstuffed station wagon facing the back window, I was anxious, yet bursting with optimism.

As the car coasted up the long stretch of road, I counted the street lines, stared at the Oklahoma cows grazing, and witnessed the sun traveling along with us. Not really understanding what was ahead, I still had a sense of excitement and wonder about this trip. To my knowledge, we had been to Tulsa before but never to live. I knew this time was different because of my mother's new sense of urgency. Her protective skills and motherly instinct had heightened to a new level, and I liked it. It was as if the lioness in her had come alive. Her love and desire to protect us had never been more evident. All I could conceive was that she was taking care of business with my brothers and me in mind.

While riding to Tulsa, I revisited that horrific conflict between my father and mother. It was devastating and forever changed me. Even though it has been over forty years since it occurred, I still hate it. Reluctantly, I found myself fixated on the thought of that violent act, causing my heart to become heavier by the mile. I was questioning why it happened while simultaneously wondering what life would have been like had my father been with us in that car. But remarkably, I changed my mental gears and chose to dream about a new place where living would be better, quieter, much more peaceful, and safer. I declared never to park my thoughts in that place of violence, chaos, and pain again. Though I was physically moving from one city to another, I had to move as well emotionally. To do that, I had to dream another dream.

Upon our arrival in Tulsa, we took up residence with my uncle, aunt, and two cousins in a small two-bedroom apartment in a government housing project. For the next several months or so, the five us shared this tiny space with the four of them. Nine people living in a two-bedroom apartment was a major shock for us all.

Now, as the sole provider, the financial struggle became the norm for my mother. The resource pool was low, and we had very few, if any, relationships of significant influence in our corner. My three brothers and I did not have the best shoes or clothing. We didn't have opportunities for cultural exposure, or any other luxuries designed to educate our minds. Opportunities such as summer camps, vacations, and many other educational resources were now out of reach.

Though experiencing struggle was common with our new move, it didn't deter my mother from serving those who were less fortunate. She never made excuses or pointed the finger at anyone to blame for her situation. Her ability to see the best in others and move beyond their mistakes overshadowed any justifiable opportunity to stay angry and disappointed.

Thus, she never stopped giving and was always available for the elderly. She served in her local church by teaching Sunday school and volunteering as the church bus driver and secretary. She offered to cook, clean apartments, and run errands for those who couldn't. Regardless of her economic status, her heart to serve never wavered.

Though we encountered all sorts of heavy conditions, my mother kept home life as light as possible, during the turbulent marriage and after the divorce. She played hide-and-go-seek in the dark with us. It was kind of scary, so we called the game "Monster." On one occasion of Monster, I ran into her big cowboy belt buckle with a fifty-cent piece set in the middle of it and knocked one of my teeth loose. And yes, I cried, but I got over it quickly because I knew the tooth fairy would soon put a quarter under my pillow.

Another source of fun was the reading sessions we had with each other. Most of the time, my oldest brother, Ray, would take the lead. On Saturday mornings, I woke up as early as six o'clock to do my chores before the highly sought-after Saturday morning cartoons. While my brothers and I watched cartoons, my mother prepared omelettes, grits, bacon, and homemade pancakes. Occasionally, a couple of our cousins would join us for pancake eating contests. I wasn't much of a participant since I could only eat about two pancakes in one sitting. But Ray and my cousin, Kenny Ray, could eat upwards of eight to ten pancakes at a time. The contest always ended up being between those two.

Because of my mother's excellent culinary skills, cooking was a big part of our lives. She always made a point to expose us to different types of foods. "I want you all to taste the unique foods of the world," she would say. We may not have had much, but occasionally, my mother sacrificed so we could experience foods like caviar, escargot, mangos, fresh coconuts, and many other exotic foods that were not common to us. I'll never forget that.

Shortly after her divorce, my mother did her best to continue her education. But while attending school, she used government assistance to provide. She eventually stopped attending classes. She thought it was conflictual to use government funds and not work. So, after quitting school, she worked a lot, doing side jobs like network marketing and other services for people.

I recall her applying permanent wave solutions to her friend's hair. Let me explain. A permanent wave solution was used to achieve the popular 1980's hairstyle known as "The

Jheri Curl." It was the same hairstyle Michael Jackson wore on the cover of his album "Thriller." After the Jheri Curl trend phased out, she began baking some of her favorite recipes and sold them for profit. She was always innovative just to make ends meet. I guess this is how I learned to get my hustle on.

I believe my mother knew life would become difficult after leaving my father. However, she thought it was better to support my brothers and me alone than to continue subjecting herself to domestic violence. And I assure you, the challenges kept flooding in with no dam to slow them down. For instance, housing and schooling options were a bit challenging. Because of the volatility, over six years, I attended six different elementary schools.

Years later, we finally settled in an area that was quite hostile. My brothers and I had to adjust quickly to this new environment. Drugs, sex, fights, and gangs had become a part of our everyday lives in just one move. There were times when we fought against a mob of guys who liked beating up on multiple people for no apparent reason. Discussion about gangs had soon become our number one topic during conversations on the playground. The second topic of choice was how we would avoid a drive-by shooting.

During our first week of living in this particular neighborhood, my younger brother and I took a walk around the corner to a park called "Chamberlain." We were having a good time until an older boy started picking on him. I intervened, asking that boy to stop. He did for the moment, and my brother and I continued to play. However, as we walked through a dense trail of trees and bushes on our way home, eight boys rushed us, and the fight was on.

Apparently, the kid didn't take too kindly to me breaking up the altercation between him and my brother earlier. So, he attacked us with what seemed like an army. However, we fought our way free and returned home. We never mentioned this to my mother because we knew things were already hard enough for her. We didn't want to add more worries to the list of demands that life had already placed on her.

Obstacles began occurring more frequently in our home. My brothers and I felt insurmountable pressure to conform just to be able to survive in our environment. It took putting up a lot of resistance not to become bitter and detached. At times, food was scarce. My mother's hand-made tortillas spread with peanut butter was often the only thing we had to eat. Though it tasted great, it quickly got old. When we didn't have transportation and utilities, it made planning everything quite tricky.

I remember the water company disconnecting our service, and we would manually turn it back on. After doing that one time too many, the water company removed the entire water meter, leaving my mother no other option but to pay the bill at the sacrifice of not paying something else. One year, we had to set out clean buckets and a large rubber trashcan to collect rainwater for drinking, flushing our toilets, and boiling so we could wash dishes.

Even though life felt intolerable at times, I was still grateful to have moved. No amount of financial or material resources could have replaced the peace we finally had. The first dream of having our whole family living a tranquil life under the same room died. But it didn't mean that life was over. It was just time to dream another dream. And because of a new dream, the struggle was worth it. As for the struggle, it did not destroy me. On the contrary, it enhanced my faith, making me more resilient.

For many years since that time, I have occasionally wondered how life would have been had my parents stayed together. I couldn't help but believe it would have been better to have them support my brothers and me. But as quickly as those thoughts come, I resettled in my mind that the old dream failed. It just didn't work out. ***Regardless of*** *whose fault it was, I couldn't change anything except dream something new.* And that new dream is still alive today. I'm living in peace despite the storms of life that continue to rage.

Each journey to our dreams and living out our purpose is unique to us. Mine started at five years old and continues to this day.

There is one thing I've learned: dreams lose their virtue unless you ENJOY the journey. Not that everything about it has to be good; it most likely won't be. But you shouldn't be consistently miserable either. *No desire is worth losing the essence of who you are.* Never pursue a dream at the risk of losing yourself. But be flexible and make the necessary adjustments to maintain your character and joy along the way.

My ambitions are important to me. How I get there and who I get there with may change. However, my desire will always remain the same: to add value to life's most exceptional beneficiaries—people. I learned that from my mother. *She was consistently the same giving, loving, and serving person regardless of her journey while simultaneously trying to resurrect her dream,* which was to keep our hope alive. With that in mind, I have the power to resurrect any dream. And if

I fail to achieve it under certain conditions, I can just dream up a new one. We are not limited to one only one dream. We can always dream another dream.

So, how can you acquire the courage to dream another dream when the first dream falls apart?

1) Resist becoming cynical. It's easy to expect the worst of people after being disappointed with those who failed you and treat possibilities with much doubt after seeing what was supposed to be a dream come true turn into an idea that died. Cynicism is the enemy of dreams. Some struggles have a way of stripping us of the child-like faith we once had. If you resist accepting your bad experiences as your destiny, you can continue to believe in people and your dreams. Though you may have physically escaped your past, you can remain emotionally imprisoned. A good start is to forgive yourself. When you let yourself off the hook, it's easy to release others as well. Then you'll be able to move on with your new dream.

2) Don't just talk about a new dream; get busy. Start by using whatever resources you already have. Abandon all of your excuses and negative thoughts. Limit associating with people that pour cold water on your dreams. This will help keep your hope alive.

"For dreams come through much effort..." (Ecclesiastes 5:3 Amplified Bible).

3) Be definite and intentional—clarify your goals and stay in your lane. Lose the idea that you can become and do anything you desire without opposition. That thought is a farce and will only lead to disappointment. Your dreams are achievable as long as you attempt to scale walls that you are meant to conquer. Remember: It's when you utilize your gifts that opportunities will come your way.

TYSON D. THOMPSON

CHAPTER FOUR:
WHAT MATTERS MOST

"Better a diamond with a flaw than a pebble without."

— Confucius

Actual value is specific to humanity even though we value lesser things like unique cars, authentic paintings, and one-of-a-kind clothing items. *Having nothing to do with personal merit, our true value is based on the simple fact that we exist, which infers that we were chosen.* As a single truth, each of us exists solely and exclusively as a one-of-a-kind. We can be identified by a single strand of hair or fingerprints though we live with billions of others on the planet. So, I think it would be fair to say that nothing in this world matters, but you and me. Unfortunately, we don't realize this until we lose each other.

During the summer of 1998, my mother's fourth child died at the young age of twenty-two. My brother, Mercury, was rushed to the hospital only to die three days later of bacterial meningitis. This tragic loss was a scenario that was now all too familiar to my mother. She tragically lost her first child, her only daughter, when she was sixteen months old after accidentally ingesting rat poison. But amazingly, she immediately sprang into action and planned my brother's funeral services. Her idea was to celebrate Mercury's life.

My brother was a unique individual— quiet, yet extremely social. He was well-known for being a great dancer and his ability to move and torque his body in ways that seemed humanly impossible. For this reason, my mother wanted to honor him by having dancing at his service.

The church was at capacity with over five hundred people in attendance. There was standing room only. I was overwhelmed with the response to this twenty-two-year-old young man's funeral service. There were people of all ages telling stories of the times they spent with him. THEY SAW HIS VALUE. To my surprise, an elderly gentleman pulled me to the side to share how he and Mercury hung out and went fishing together. He praised my brother's kindness towards him, expressing what a joy he was to be around. What a celebration it was.

I do not doubt that my mother loves my two remaining siblings and me. But we can never replace her daughter and the son who passed on. I wouldn't dare try to relate to her loss or any other parent who prematurely lost a child. But it's clear how precious their lives were. My mother taught us that life is a gift, and true value only exists in life's greatest recipients: PEOPLE. And I repeat, to truly value others, one must first value SELF.

When my mother lost her first child and only daughter, who was sixteen months old, she was devastated. She was angry at God as she blamed Him for her death. She fell into a state of depression, which became unbearable that she admitted herself into a medical facility. Medications prescribed for her kept her so depressed that she had to stop working and drop out of school. The depression continued to worsen, but she eventually found the strength to taper off the medications.

She slowly gathered herself and vowed to move forward with her life. She reminded herself that people are most important, which included herself. She was determined not to allow grief to rob her of living a life that could add value to others. My mother later gave birth to four more children to love and care for.

When I think of my two deceased siblings, I can't help but think of their significance even though their lives were cut short. We'll never know the extent to which their contributions would have impacted this world. The almost sixteen months of my sister's life created memories for my mother that can't be erased. My brother's twenty-two years meant so much to so many people as we saw at his homegoing. So, I often revisit the concept that the people involved in my life are most important, despite how long I have them, and despite their mistakes. Once they are gone, their mistakes no longer matter anyway.

As my resolve is continuously tested, I think about my father, who wasn't given the privilege of choosing his parents, as none of us were. It wasn't his choice to be born into his situation. He didn't arrive on this planet of his own free will, and neither did I. Therefore, I found it to be more beneficial to my life to adopt the philosophy that I should be humble as I journey through life. I've been gifted with a wonderful opportunity to experience the best this life has to offer. But I must also face the inevitable trials that come with it.

At funerals, no one mentions the mistakes of the deceased—everyone only mentions the good. We are all perfectly human and subject to failure because we are also humanly flawed. Our flaws often put a damper on our ability to nurture our relationships. But since we are recipients of this gift of life, I choose to embrace it and make the best of it, flaws and all. I've committed never to lose sight of the truth about what matters most: people. ***Though my inherent value can never be questioned, my unwillingness to acknowledge or add value to others can.*** I firmly believe I've been given the privilege of living, and with that privilege, I'm equipped with the intangibles which empower me to help others. ***Therefore, my purpose in life is not only to see the value in people but also to add value to people. It's your purpose as well.***

How to Begin Valuing What Matters Most

1) *Believe in people.* As I strive to fulfill my dreams, it's apparent that people are the only assets I can't live without, flaws and all. Seeing how I can never be fulfilled alone, I need them; so do you. For this reason, we can't give up on each other. Besides, each other is all we have.

2) *Serve people.* As humans, we have a civil and social obligation to grow and develop

to add value to others. Use your exceptional talents to solve problems, not create them. Even though you may not always please people, you can still serve them.

3) *Honor people.* Think about this. In general, your home, car, watch, designer bag, business, and other tangible items can be replaced, remade, or rebuilt. However, once a grandmother, aunt, sister, father, or someone else passes, they never return to this life. We are originals, and therefore, priceless.

CHAPTER FIVE:
COURAGE: SECURING YOUR VALUE

"Speak up, the world awaits your value."

— Tyson D. Thompson

You were born with the highest value a human can possess. You made your grand entrance into this world with gifts, talents, and a purpose before you could second guess whether you were worthy or not. Your young mind was free from cynicism or negative thinking. There was no understanding of the meaning of the word "can't."

Since your birth, your value hasn't diminished. But due

to life's unwarranted challenges, that may be hard to believe. Possibly distracted by the world's system that rates you based on your ethnicity, zip code, appearance, economic status, popularity, and past failures. Unfortunately, you may have made the mistake of buying into it and began judging yourself accordingly. If that's the case, you can change. It's not what "they" say and believe about you that matters; it's what "you," say, and think about yourself that has the most significant impact on your life. All you may need is a little COURAGE.

The origin of the word courage comes from a Latin word cor meaning heart. The original definition is "tell the story of who you are with your whole heart." With many of us unsure of who we indeed are, genuinely communicating can be a daunting task. In my case, I masked my true identity as an attempt to please my colleagues, family, and friends for years— finally losing my individuality. I struggled to lead with confidence. For some reason, I would conceal my ideas and never share my true beliefs. During conflict, I often retreated to keep the peace, hoping others would affirm me'. That didn't work. My lack of confidence pushed people further away. Eventually, I no longer dared to speak up. I had become a fraud.

Although I was not intentionally lying, it didn't pardon me from the consequences of fraudulent behavior (I'll disclose more in a later chapter). Frustrated, I eventually lost interest in responding to others' concerns— becoming deaf to their deep issues— sabotaging any influence I may have gained in their lives. Eager for approval, my behavior was often shifty and impulsive. My unwillingness to make defining decisions negatively affected my business and my ability to focus, double-minded I had become.

In 2005 I relocated my business. I hired a local contractor to do the buildout. He was an energetic guy with the gift of gab. After going over the plans in detail, he was a little agitated. That should have been my first clue that he was a disaster waiting to happen. He was an awful listener. He was so eager to get to work that he ignored those details I laid out. But I was a fool. I didn't adhere to my gut feeling that he wasn't the guy for my project. Eventually, he over-promised and underdelivered.

After the first two weeks of construction, I wasn't pleased. I told the contractor of my concerns, but he assured me things were going beautifully. Two weeks later, there were no signs of change. Embarrassingly, I didn't speak up. Because he had shared that his family was having a tough time, I gave him a pass. So, to spare his feelings, I held back on my request, hoping things would magically fall in place. What a failure in leadership that was.

Soon the project fell behind. And after my final inspection, I learned that my contractor had never applied for a city work permit. And because of that, we started the project uninformed. The inspector enlightened me that I needed a second bathroom to meet code based on my square footage. That cost me an additional $5,000 and shut down my re-grand opening. Though the amount of money wasn't a major loss, the influence I forfeited was priceless. My staff at the time lost a little respect for me. With just cause, they questioned my leadership. This inconvenience could have been avoided had I spoken up and held my contractor accountable. But out of fear, I was silent. While, that mistake cost me significantly, I still had not learned my lesson yet.

About seven years later, in my car, I contemplated my next career move while sitting in front of a local restaurant. I was going back and forth in my mind if I was capable of completing what I knew to be true. As I prayed for clarity, I became fearful. It was clear that I was meant to write, educate and inspire people and their organizations. However, I discounted my abilities.

After about 10 minutes of thinking, I entered the restaurant. Little did I know a mentor of mine was standing waiting. Her name is Colleen Payne—a phenomenal businesswoman. She's the author of the book, "I Did It My Way and... It Worked!" After walking into the restaurant, I greeted her with a hug. She said, "I was thinking of you. I remember you telling me about your project. How's it going?" Unconsciously, I began to give her excuses as to why I had not completed my next steps. Well, my rambling didn't satisfy her. Colleen is a very assertive individual—she holds no punches. She looked me in the eyes and told me this,

> *"Tyson, if you don't speak up about the little black boy with a dream, no one will ever hear about him. The only way you're going to make it is to be bold about who you are. I'm not successful because of someone else. I spoke up about who I was and what I was capable of doing for people. You have to do the same. No one's going to give it to you. You have to go get it."*

Her words of wisdom changed my life.

I encourage you, if you intend to CHOOSE YOUR FUTURE, CONQUER YOUR PAST, AND LEAD WITH

CONFIDENCE, you have to speak up! You must secure your value. Trust me; it's a lesson I learned the hard way. Be courageous and learn to share your heart compassionately as long as your motive is to add value to others. Your sharing is essential because we all must bring relief to humanity. What is more, as you deliver assistance to those in need, you will soon discover another level of satisfaction in life you may have been desiring.

Is it clear to you now that there is nothing wrong when someone safeguards their worth? By doing so, the people you care about will not become lessened. Keep in mind; their value is inherent also. But if you diminish the value you have to share with the world, you may deplete the world of what's necessary.

I genuinely believe I was created with intent, whether anyone believes that or not. Besides, life chose me, gave me purpose, which indicates that I have value. No individual, private failure, unforeseen circumstance, or a negative mindset can take it away. Can you see your worth in its entirety now? I hope so because we need you— the world awaits your value.

When I'm having moments of apprehension, I do a few things to acknowledge my value. I hope you consider adopting these principles for yourself.

1) Embrace life and each day as a gift, considering it's the only life you have. Even if it's not the life you would have chosen, be grateful. Today, if you are breathing and in your right mind, you have the opportunity to make it better. So, gain more knowledge, learn new strategies, connect with positive individuals, and give thanks for your life as it is, believing it can be what you desire it to be.

2) Show yourself some appreciation. Treat yourself with the same love and respect you give to others. Take some time each day to think about all of your attributes and strengths. What things do people appreciate most about you? Write them down. Looked them over daily. Then appreciate yourself for those same things, and more.

3) Change what you don't like. Don't just wish. Even if you don't have the means or knowledge to change everything at this point, you can change something. Start with making the right choices for yourself, even if the right decisions make you cringe

or disappoint others. Stay focused on the desired end. Do all you can to be your best for you and everyone in your life.

4) Be humble, transparent, and vulnerable to those close to you. Look beyond yourself and be open to constructive criticism. Allow them to share openly about your strengths and shortcomings. Give them access to your heart so that you can correct any behaviors or ideas that can prevent you from valuing yourself and those around you. Don't let pride separate you from the people you love.

5) Preserve your life by guarding your heart, developing your mind, and nurturing your body. By investing in yourself, you are also indirectly investing in others. You will then be prepared to preserve the best of humanity.

6) Enjoy your life. Discover new things. Develop your skills. Pursue your passion. Expand your territory. Explore new relationships. Don't shy away from new challenges—probe new opportunities. Share your life by serving others.

CHAPTER SIX:
A LOVE STORY

"This is love: not that we loved God,
but that he loved us"

— I John 4:10 (New International Version)

LOVE is the single most powerful influence that has ever existed; however, its impact is highly underestimated. We often resort to everything else first because loving in unlovely circumstances costs us something: pride. It's almost impossible to give love that can preserve humanity while being too focused on self-preservation. Love that has to be earned isn't love at all. An essential part of self-preservation is to love without condition. It does just as much for us as it does for those with whom we share it.

I was thirteen years old when my father moved in with us for about a month; he had diabetes. I didn't see him that often, so I was a little unnerved. Plus, witnessing him take his insulin shots was a bit creepy. However, I have to admit it was a little weird having him there. I wasn't quite sure where the relationship was going.

While my father was living with us, one of my fondest memories was watching him cook sunny side up eggs and steak for breakfast. Until that time, I didn't recall ever trying sunny side up eggs. But after I observed him cooking it for the first time, I've been a fan ever since.

Less than two years later, he was placed in a rehabilitation center. But after many years of continuous alcohol and drug abuse and fighting diabetes, he eventually slipped into a diabetic coma. My father died just before a scheduled amputation of his foot when I was fifteen years old. Regrettably, I was very disconnected from him and didn't attend his funeral. That's something I'm not very proud of.

Though my mother suffered abuse at my father's hand for many years, before his death, she visited him in the hospital to encourage and pray for him. Regardless of their rocky past, it was amazing how she never stopped loving him. She may not have been romantically in love with him, but she loved him unconditionally.

My mother had a similar experience with my grandfather, who rejected her for years, refusing to be a part of her life. When she was a young girl, he lived across the street from her but would only visit when she was sick. His comments to her during those times were very insensitive. "You need to get it together," he would say to her.

When I was about eight years old, my grandfather turned down my mother's offer to get to know my brothers and me better. After she proposed the idea, he told her, "I would like to keep things the way they are." So, not only did he reject her, he openly rejected her children as well. Nonetheless, despite being stressed and even suffering bouts of depression as a result of her father's rejection—first at eight years old, and again as a teenager—my mother spent the final years of his life caring for him. This behavior was real love in action.

I was ecstatic for my mother because I knew firsthand what this meant to her. As a young boy, I remember her sitting on the edge of her bed crying because the pain of her father's neglect troubled her. I'm not sure if she ever got over it. But while he still had breath in his body, she continued to put her father's needs above her feelings. His value as a person and as my grandfather was more important to her than her pain. Her dream of having a father who would embrace and love her never happened. So, it was apparent that she had to *DREAM ANOTHER DREAM* and make herself a part of his life by taking care of him. She chose to value whatever relationship she could have with him.

I'm not sure if my mother continued hoping or had given up on the possibility of having a healthy relationship with her father. But I'm sure she didn't predict what would come years later even though a relative shared with my mother the countless conversations they had with her father about treating my mother with respect. They discussed the likelihood of him needing my mother to take care of him in the future. Coincidence or not, the last three years of my grandfather's life was a dream come true for her.

We had incredible holidays together with my grandfather, eating dinner and watching television. I remember how he teased my mother about the Jerry Springer Show. He loved that show. He jokingly laughed at how she didn't know anything about it, inferring it was too much for her to handle. My mother enjoyed that. But what blessed her most was witnessing her father playing with his great-grandchildren since he had never played with my brothers or me when we were kids. So, this was monumental for her, nothing short of a miracle.

You may be wondering how anyone could demonstrate this type of honor and respect for a person that treated them with such disregard. That's very understandable but let me explain. The secret is simple: LOVE FIRST. That's how my mother was able to be faithful to her principles after many years of blatant neglect. She demonstrated the "Agape" type of love, a love that is unconditional and unwavering, not based on emotions, feelings, or circumstances.

Basically, the love of God is a selfless love that never changes. It exceeds all other forms of human love. The very essence of this kind of love is by nature, love itself as it is characterized by patience, kindness, faithfulness, gentleness, correction, and even justice. When this brand of love is trusted, it can empower anyone to be emotionally free from injustices inflicted on them and their most painful memories. Loving her father with this untainted level of love is how she reclaimed her soul.

Generally speaking, love is commonly referred to as just a feeling or a deep emotion, typically affiliated with romance or the motivating factor behind a nurturing mother or father. These have become accepted definitions of love, but they fall short since they are affiliated with the human experience. And depending on an individual's emotional response to certain life events, their perception of love may be skewed. In cases where an enraged, jealous lover harms the very object of his affection, or an obsessive mother defends her guilty son who is a rapist, or an abused child becomes an adult and trusts no one, "love" is dangerously misrepresented. Love that's driven by control, fear, or intimidation has neither power to heal nor sustain, and therefore, can't be trusted.

As a community activist working with troubled teens, I have seen firsthand how love can be misconstrued, often swaying people to be loving only if their material or emotional expectations are met. I recall how one of the juveniles I counseled would manipulate his grandmother to bring illegal contraband during visits at the Lloyd E. Rader Center. If she didn't comply, he would belligerently accuse her of not loving him while blaming her for his problems. He would also physically assault her during her next visit with him and then threaten to do even worse when he was released from custody. But ironically, he would fight to protect her if anyone attempted to harm her. Sadly, out of fear, his grandmother would continuously give in to his warped demands.

Clearly, this level of love is immature and unreliable—defiantly one-sided and driven by insecurity, selfishness, fear, and pride. And I assure you, it will turn its back on anyone who attempts to trust it. Like a thief in the night, this toxic love will catch you off-guard. While it will not come for external accomplishments, it can negatively affect them. After successfully sucking you in, it will rob you of what matters most: relationships of great value. No one should ever settle for such a love. It does more damage than good.

My mother had just cause to be angry towards her father and my dad. And I'm sure you feel justified to demand retribution and payback for the hell someone sent you through. But I warn you: don't fall for that trap! An eye for an eye will only start a trend of repeated cycles of more dysfunction in your life. Until justice can be served, adopt a perspective of love. *It may not change your adversary or your circumstances, but it will commence your healing and give you the peace of mind you'll need while navigating through tough times.*

In retrospect, choosing to love my father empowered me to honor him though he was unwilling to care for me. And with that power, I became free emotionally, physically, and spiritually to enjoy my life without him. Choosing to love him unconditionally didn't mean becoming his doormat. By no means should anyone live in harm's way. I didn't want to relive what he had put us through daily because it would have imprisoned me, isolating me from the relationships that mattered most. There had to be a healthy distance between us, which would allow me to grow into the person I needed to be.

I've accepted the fact that I live in an unfair world occupied by malicious-minded individuals. However, to make it better, I must continue to acknowledge the best in people regardless of who they are and what they do. True love has now become the foundation of all my relationships. It empowers me to believe in others regardless of their flaws. Thus, I can effectively lead others without being judgmental and love them recklessly without regret.

As I wake up daily to the grind of life, it is apparent that *people are the only real assets I can't live without.* As a matter of fact, I never have and never will exist without them. So, I strive to cherish all my relationships on all levels. Their value is significant in my life and far surpasses the value of anything I could ever possess. I acknowledge that I could never become my best self alone; I need people. Therefore, I can't give up on them. I know there's a potential for being treated with disloyalty, but relationships are worth the risk because they are too necessary to avoid or take for granted.

I want to challenge you to live consistently with an Agape love because it's your only hope. Harboring resentment will only eat away at you and cloud your judgment of good-hearted people who never have or will intentionally hurt you. I'm a living witness! If you choose to trust in true love, you will not be disappointed because true love never fails.

Here's what you can do to up your "love game."

1) Adjust your lens and choose to look beyond people's exterior to see the good in them. The first part of John 3:16 (King James Version) says, "For God so loved the world, that He gave his only begotten Son. ." This passage demonstrates how the undeserving—which includes all of us—need the Agape love that can reach our hearts and change our lives. When you let people know they are worth real love, they may begin to love themselves and others. Initiate the cycle. True love responds first.

2) Love first. Agape love isn't the level of

love widely used. Some will be suspicious of unconditional love, undeserved, patient, kind, thoughtful, humble, polite, temperate, forgiving, protective, and courteous. But don't let their initial reaction discourage you. Sometimes, you must press beyond their resistance.

3) Manage your expectations. People are not perfect; none of us are. Therefore, you may need the grace to deal with those who have mistreated you. Be discerning and pump the brakes if necessary. Remember: We are perfectly human, yet humanly flawed. Sometimes you must love people from a distance. Forgive them. It is for your benefit so you can free up space in your heart to love unconditionally.

4) Be valuable. True love is expressed through selfless and unconditional conduct and service. Adding value to others will reduce those lonely moments of self-pity, regret, and fear. Redirecting your energy towards a more significant cause will put you one step closer to your DREAMS.

CHAPTER SEVEN:
THOUGHTS

"A man is literally what he thinks, his character being
the complete sum of all his thoughts."

–James Allen

I want to start this chapter off with a childhood story. I
believe you will get the message and can relate it to some
part of your life.

One hot summer day in 1981, the playground where
we lived was crowded with kids ready to play "tag." Tag is
a playground game of cat and mouse where one kid chases
the rest of the kids until they catch one. Once the chaser
catches someone, they are supposed to yell, "You're it!" It then

becomes that kid's turn to chase the other kids until one is caught. I couldn't wait to get out there with them. I darted out of the apartment building, letting the squeaky screen door slam behind me. I was only seven years old when I ran as fast as I could to the large grungy playground so I could take part in the game.

Once the game started, I was tagged relatively quickly, mainly due to my lack of speed. Back then, I was as slow as a turtle. But it was my turn to tag someone, so the chase was on! Everyone immediately scattered. As I chased after my buddies, my slow rate of speed became very obvious. I know I said I was as slow as a turtle, but it's more like tree sap seeping from a tree on a cold day. It wasn't long before all the kids laughed at me, including my older brother, Ray.

One guy named Patrick was laughing the hardest. He was short, lean, and as quick as a rabbit. He kind of looked like Stephen Curry, the superstar point guard of the NBA. And to make matters worse, he had a high squeaky voice, which made his taunting of me very disturbing. I was offended, so I decided he was going to be tagged first. But to this very day, I question why I did that, considering how slow I was. But that didn't stop me from trying. At one point, I thought I had Patrick trapped, but he ran left and right so fast that he made me trip. As I picked myself up from the ground, the other kids were bent over in tears cracking up. I must say, with laughs like that, winning America's Got Talent would have been a sure victory for me. But I digress.

Out of desperation and pride, I dusted off my clothes, picked the gravel from my little afro, and geared up one more time to catch Patrick. Still, I just couldn't catch up with him. The longer he ran, the more irritated I became, which only fueled his laughter. It wasn't long before I was uninspired to try to catch anyone. Heck, I could hardly catch my breath! The hot Oklahoma sun beamed down on my forehead, causing sweat to drip from my pointed eyebrows; exhaustion had set in. Humiliated by the kids' constant laughter and teasing, I suddenly screamed out of frustration, "I quit!"

Tired and embarrassed, I ran as fast as I could towards our apartment building to tell my mother what happened. Not only was I embarrassed, but I was also eager to escape the commotion. It was as if a pack of wild hyenas was chasing me. I could hear the echoes of all the kids heckling and laughing, mainly Patrick.

When I reached the back porch, I swung open the tattered screen door and stormed into the apartment crying at the top of my lungs, "Mama, Mama!" And in a flash, she seemingly appeared out of thin air. Like most caring mothers, she asked, "What's wrong, baby?" After what felt like an eternity of huffing and puffing, I finally caught my breath enough to speak. I began telling her how sad I was because I couldn't catch Patrick while playing tag. I also shared with her how all the kids laughed at me because I was too slow to catch him.

While spilling my guts to her, I could feel the weight of the moment slowly lifting away. I anticipated her loving arms flying open to grab and console me. And I could hardly wait because she has never let me down. But to my surprise, instead of embracing and comforting me, my mother spanked and scolded me. While swinging away on me, she said, "I don't want to hear you crying because people laughed at you, Tyson! You can't control what they think, but you can control how you think and feel. So, get it together and stop crying before I give you something to cry about. Do you understand me?" I responded, "Yes, Mama." That was a pivotal moment I would never forget.

However, for a brief moment, I was puzzled. I thought, Man, I didn't do anything wrong. Those kids were all laughing at me, even my brother. And all I wanted was a little love. Though I was still a little bit taken back by my mother's response, I instantly came to my senses. My young adolescent mind knew that she loved me, and since she had never failed me, I trusted her. She had never given me any reason to doubt her. So, after sniffing, wiping my face, and clearing my throat, I began to understand. I suddenly realized my mother might have been on to something as this situation wasn't worth me shedding tears over.

After some reflection, I soon began to appreciate the lesson my mother wanted me to learn. It was neither about a mere game of tag nor the kids' laughter. She knew that the world was cruel, lacked compassion, and would offer me little to no mercy. For that reason, her philosophy was to strengthen me inwardly.

Today, I refer to that inward strengthening as posturing, a term I picked up from my good friend and business partner, Chris Staten. I understood it to mean "maintaining a strong internal attitude of confidence despite any outside influences," though it may not be the exact definition. Albert Einstein shared the same idea as he stated: *"Great spirits have always encountered violent opposition from mediocre minds."* I came to terms with the fact that I was the one who needed to change. Almost immediately, I noticed how my thoughts about myself had more power over me than the kids' thoughts on the playground.

After finishing my first "personal development meeting" with my mother, I took a few swigs of cherry-flavored Kool-Aid ® (we called it "red" Kool-Aid®) to wash the taste of salty tears from my mouth. I took a few deep breaths, and reluctantly returned to the playground. As I approached the field, I heard a kid yelling, "There he is!" Immediately, the laughter and name-calling began. Somehow, I gathered the COURAGE to ignore the demeaning remarks and took my position as the chaser by allowing myself to be tagged.

Once tagged, I had a new strategy: to tag whoever I could. But first, I gave tagging Patrick another shot, but I failed miserably. Although I gave it my all, I just wasn't fast enough, or he was just too swift. And of course, they laughed even more than before. But instead of allowing it to bother me, I swallowed my pride and chose to continue to enjoy the game. After all, it was just a game.

It was evident to the kids on the playground that I hadn't changed physically. I still had on my beat up, bubble gum Nike athletic shoes, wore a shaggy afro hairstyle, and had relatively short legs. Though I was still slower than a farm tractor traveling on a busy city street, that day, I refused to identify with being a failure. My thinking matured rather quickly.

I was grateful to discover many years later that my new outlook on life was that of many successful individuals. The philosophy of right-thinking wasn't new at all. However, though not new, the topic will always remain relevant because many people still fail to embrace the concept of thinking and meditating positively. I believe it is the foundation for living well. In the inspirational classic, *"Think and Grow Rich,"* Napoleon Hill says this:

> *You have absolute control over but one thing, and that is your thoughts. This is the most significant and inspiring of all facts known to man! It reflects man's divine nature. This divine prerogative is the sole means by which you may control your own destiny. If you fail to control your own mind, you may be sure you will control nothing else. If you must be careless with your possessions, let it be in connection with material things. Your mind is your spiritual estate! Protect and use it with the care to which divine royalty is entitled. You were given a willpower for this purpose.*

Everyone's story is unique to them; individual struggles are very personal. But trials are part of the human experience that no one can escape. And wrong thinking will always be the detrimental factor which hinders us from responding to tough times appropriately. I wouldn't dare suggest that wrong thinking is the cause of all of our troubles, but it impacts the outcomes. A habit of negative thinking ultimately affects our core belief system, which affects our behavior, health, and what we believe about ourselves. We become our most dominant thoughts.

It was on January 18, 2019—exactly four days before my forty-fifth birthday—when I finally accepted the idea that it is my responsibility to manage my own human experience. Everyone else is expected to do the same. Coming to this conclusion was significant for me because, for years, I felt overly obligated to succumb to other people's wishes and opinions of me. Though I dealt with the "Patrick" situation that day on the playground, it seemed like a spirit of failure had a bounty on my soul like an arch enemy committed to plaguing me for life. Consequently, it took my entire life until that day in January to rid my thoughts of the harmful residue left behind from years of disbelief and self-doubt.

Exhaustingly, I had to fight many internal demons to reclaim my birthright—to dream big. There were times I thought of giving up. For years, I regrettably made stupid excuses for why I could not do my thing—a thing like write this book– while others delivered their value to the world. I deemed myself a simple barber with no formal education or credentials that amounted to much. I habitually discounted my ideas and aspirations. My thinking was toxic. But it's funny that no one noticed my true feelings due to my many accomplishments.

> *Hidden beneath my spirited demeanor was a self-image so twisted, I emotionally sidelined myself and sat on the bench while disregarding the call on my life.* ***Even though significant opportunities were all around me, I failed to act on any of them because I wasn't willing to face the emotional mountain that I dreaded climbing—rejection.*** *I was terrified of not being able to live up to people's expectations. Their thoughts and opinions overshadowed my passions like a black cloak only to conceal my true identity.*

I'm excited to share that I know better now. I'm fortunate to have learned the lessons embedded within this dilemma. No explanations for cynical thinking will pardon me from the consequences of remaining irrationally dysfunctional. In other words, NO EXCUSES! I know better now. *I will no longer apologize for being my best self. And if someone tries to put me in a box, I know not to get in.*

Regardless of whether I had a dysfunctional past or not, at some point, I had to take control of my soul and not give its jurisdiction to what I can't possibly manage: others' thoughts and emotions. Think about it. We are all in the same boat. Our parents, spouses, friends, communities, the government, or even our bosses can no longer be the scapegoat for our lack of achievements. We can only be bound by our self-imposed limitations.

It's a fact; none of us chose the lives we were given as children. So, it is a waste of time nagging and complaining about it. Besides, we cannot change anything that has already happened; *we can only make corrections in our present moment and influence our future.*

If you can somehow miraculously find tickets to the past, I'll front you the cash to buy them and we can go together. We could then make modifications to our parents or even swap them out for new ones. Perhaps, we could decline that regretful marriage proposal or choose a different career path. Maybe it will be possible to undo every negative thing that has happened to us like the abuse we went through, what our fathers did, what our mothers said, or how kids in school humiliated us for their enjoyment. Maybe you can help me catch "Patrick" and stop the laughing that still attempts to annoy me to this day.

So, what do you say? Should we pack our bags? I'm ready to go if you are since it's been a dream of mine to correct the wrongs done to all of humanity for years. Well, we both know the truth: we can't return to the past. But our adverse history cannot follow us into our future unless we choose to bring it with us.

It's clear to me now that I may never catch up with my personal "Patrick" and stop them from harassing me. So, what! That's life. ***But in every situation, on any given day, I am blessed with the privilege of dreaming new dreams—it starts with controlling my thoughts.*** How I choose to believe about myself, and how I respond to adversity and unfavorable conditions empowers me to ascend to my highest desires and destroy barriers I am supposed to conquer. What will you do? Keep in mind that when you decide to think either small or BIG, the price will be the same: your LIFE. Think about it!

Are you ready to recondition your thoughts? If so, I challenge you to heed these following points:

1) Choose a belief system with a successful track record. Please pay attention to those who enjoy continuous success in every area of their life. Study them. Notice how they respond to challenges. Let them be your example.

2) Guard your ears. Your ears are one of the gates to your temple, and whatever enters them repeatedly will make its way to your spirit. What you hear regularly will shape your core belief system–good or bad– will direct your actions. *Your dominant thoughts will determine your outcome.*

3) Govern your words. Words have creative power and will form your perception of the world around you. They determine how you think, feel, and behave. What was spoken to you and internalized molded your life. But what you currently talk to yourself about will guide your thoughts, and ultimately, your future.

4) Train your eyes. We all have a subconscious mind that stores good and bad images. This part of the brain does not filter what is true or false, reality, or fiction. It replays only what it sees. Giving validity to the phrase, "monkey see, monkey do."

5) Meditate. Meditation is excellent for relaxing, reconditioning your thoughts, and refueling your spirit. Think on purpose instead of letting your mind wander. Please choose what you will think about and dwell on it for a few minutes several times a day.

6) Manage your relationships. Choose your friends; don't let them choose you. Protect your time and space from anyone who can potentially get you off track. Your eyes, ears, and mind are yours to protect. Love everyone but be careful to surround yourself with like-minded individuals while renewing your thoughts. "Iron sharpens iron..." (Proverbs 27:17 New International Version).

TYSON D. THOMPSON

CHAPTER EIGHT:
THE CHOICE IS YOURS

"Life is a matter of choices, and every choice you
make makes you."

—John C. Maxwell

Life is the greatest of all gifts. For without it, everything else is irrelevant. But I'd say that the second most exceptional gift is our God-given ability to CHOOSE. Plus, until we are mature enough to make critical choices, we are still given the ability to choose to submit to those responsible for us. Even as infants, we decide whether we're going to fight sleep or just give in to it. As adults, more than anything else, we repeatedly make choices throughout the day, both big and small. Pay attention to all the choices you make, starting with the minute you open your eyes tomorrow morning. You will be shocked.

Why am I making such a big deal about choices? It is the single most powerful thing we can do to either build our lives or destroy it. I want you to be conscious of how many choices you make from the moment you open your eyes until you go to bed at night because I want you to KNOW that they were all YOURS to make. Most of your outcomes are the result of decisions and beliefs. The gift of choice is liberating. You can't control others, but you can control yourself. And with liberty comes responsibility.

In 2008, I encountered a young man who gave me a greater appreciation for my strict but liberating upbringing. During my fifteen-year tenure, from 1993-2009, at the Lloyd E. Rader Treatment Center in Sand Springs, Oklahoma. Lloyd E. Rader was a diagnostic treatment center for juvenile offenders. The young men and women there had committed heinous crimes such as murder, rape, armed robbery, theft, and arson, just to name a few.

During my time there, I was fortunate to teach a curriculum I developed shortly after graduating from a small seminary school in Tulsa, Oklahoma. The curriculum helped the young offenders identify their strengths, correct their behavior, and maximize their self-worth. I served in two positions: the resident barber and a behavior coach twice a week. I spent hours attending to their needs during behavior-training sessions.

After a very intense group session, one of the juveniles decided to share his skills as a hip-hop rapper. To keep his identity safe, I will refer to him as "Tre'." Tre' was very gifted at putting words together with an effortless flow. However, I noticed that his content was very negative. The words were so negative, making his art form difficult for me to enjoy. The language he used was vulgar, violent, and degrading to women. So, I asked, "Tre', is it possible for you to rap about something more positive? If so, will you give it a try for me?" With no hesitation, Tre' shouted to one of his peers, "Give me a beat!"

As the beat dropped, he instantly began to tap his feet and snap his fingers. I just knew he was about to put on a show. But after a minute of rocking back and forth, he suddenly stopped and began to ponder, which seemed like forever. As time went on, he became agitated. I became a little nervous, considering how some of the kids would frequently have violent outbursts over the smallest issues.

Without warning, his legs were shaking, and his head swayed back and forth out of frustration. He looked up to the sky to retrieve lyrics from God knows where and let out an exhausting gasp. He gazed around the room at his peers, and with a smug look on his face, he said,

"I can't." I responded, "What do you mean you can't?"

He said, "I just can't."

"Why not?" I replied.

He said, "Mr. Tyson, if I knew something positive, I would rap about it. But I don't know anything positive. What I rap about is what I know. It's what I lived. That's all I got."

It became evident to me that Tre' was limited. He was emotionally bent towards an external perspective of control. He believed that he had no choice in the matter. Sadly, he was a victim of his environment. But in his defense, one could argue that it's not fair because his upbringing was undeniably one-sided, and his options were few. This young man was persuaded that his destructive approach towards life was typical. But regardless of his childhood, his ignorance didn't pardon him from the consequences of his behavior. His choices placed him behind bars, leaving no one to blame but himself.

That conversation sent me drifting down memory lane into my past. Statistically, I would have been doomed if I had continued to live under my father's roof. My fate would have been similar to Tre's. Laziness, double-dealing, drug abuse, womanizing, and many other dysfunctional behaviors would have been almost inevitable. As a matter of fact, the three children that lived with my father for a significant amount of time served or are currently serving prison sentences. I'm not sure what would have become of me, but the example before me wasn't promising.

That was one of the primary reasons my mother left my father; she wanted to display an alternate way of living. She demonstrated how I could choose not to respond to life the same way he did. She instilled in me that, as a young African American male, I was no different than any other red-blooded American born with a human will to choose.

During the spring of 1994, I felt like I was under constant scrutiny and pressure to be like everyone else. But my mother's principles had already been planted in me. It had already begun sprouting several years prior, but it was time to receive the harvest of my desires. I decided to go against the odds and choose an unlikely path that would open up more opportunities than I could count. And yes, I somehow managed to offend a few people along the way.

It all started with a conference hosted by Dr. Bob Harrison, also known as "Dr. Increase." He was responsible for bailing out a major Chrysler dealership in California during the 1970's gas crisis. Since that time, he has sold out arenas worldwide, sharing his message of increase. During this conference, Dr. Harrison revealed a lesson he learned after scheduling a simple haircut appointment. I'm a master barber and instructor by trade; thus, his story applied to my current situation.

While walking to his appointment, he noticed another barber company with three empty barber chairs, no patrons, a sign reading "$8 Haircuts," and a barber waiting to serve someone. He asked himself, "Why did I make a haircut appointment two weeks in advance and am willing to pay more than double for what could be the same service?" After a moment of deliberating, his answer was, "One company changed, becoming more relevant, while the other remained the same."

Simple story, right? Not for me. At the time, I was thirsting for something different. Eagerly awaiting change, I regularly shared ideas with my family and friends. But the problem was that I was surrounded by men and women who possessed a scarcity mentality and had little to no ambition to do anything to change their circumstances. I couldn't understand why anyone would refuse to grow. I was sick of being broke and under-resourced. I wanted to travel, see the world, and help people as I lived the dream. But sadly, I was often alone in my efforts.

Due to the deprivation of mutual inspiration, I eagerly made my way to Dr. Harrison's book table and purchased materials immediately after hearing his advice on "change." By the way, his book and set of twelve cassette tapes were punished by me. By the time I got done, the book cover was not legible, and the cassette tapes were falling apart. Need I say more? That day, my spiritual eyes were opened to a world of ideas I had never imagined. The concept of change consumed my thoughts with more vigor than ever. I had a restless night after I heard his simplistic, yet powerful message. And after a few days of meditating on it, I chose to take action.

At the age of twenty, after successfully being
in business for five years, I decided to relocate

to a different part of the city referred to as "the White side of town." Moving was a big deal because of my city's dark history. In 1921, there was a horrible massacre in Tulsa, Oklahoma that destroyed an area called "Black Wall Street." Black Wall Street was one of the few thriving, self-sufficient communities occupied and ran by Black Americans, discrediting the idea that people of Negro descent were incapable of social and economic advancement. Supposedly, the dollar had circulated more than thirty times before it left its people. I honestly believe that this tragic event left a wound of oppression that has yet to heal completely. As of today, one of my childhood stomping grounds still struggles for economic and social change.

Adhering to what I gleaned from Dr. Harrison's teaching, I came up with an innovative idea that was a risk worth taking. I refused to live behind that old veil of oppression, which covered the truth about my people. My strategy was to flip the script and open the doors of my business to multiple ethnicities and grow a broader clientele base. I would also implement an appointment system, start a membership plan, and raise my prices. And the expected results were diversity, more significant connections, and obviously, "Mo' Money, Mo' Money, Mo' Money!"

Sadly, my vision was misunderstood by people in my circle who shot my ideas down as quickly as I could share them. I was told as a young black man, that I was thinking too big. I wasn't allowed to think outside the box. "What more do you want? You should just stay in your place. Isn't what you have good enough?" Apparently, there was a "system" that would not allow me the pleasure of dreaming too big. "The Man will not let you succeed," some said.

For those who may not be familiar with the term, "The Man," let me explain. It's a term used to describe an economic system designed by an oppressive group of people to disenfranchise another group. For example, slavery in America was followed by Jim Crow laws, perpetuating the same system of slavery through politics, law enforcement, corporations, school systems, and other institutions. This approach was intended to be more subtle than the physical chains of slavery.

During this experience, I began to think my name was "You Can't" because that was the trending response I got from everyone with whom I shared my vision. But it was too late. My mind was made up. And as far as I was concerned, the change happened the day I heard Bob's message. Since that day, I refused to let others' low perspective of thinking stop me. I moved anyway and soon discovered that the path of least resistance is for the faint of heart, not committed DREAMERS. Some moves require moving beyond the status quo. For me, this dream demanded that I blaze a new trail.

Since my first move, I have expanded four times, remodeled twice at each location and acquired a business partner of exceptional character to help continue the dream. Today, my company is still thriving by helping young men and women develop the essential attributes required to beat the social and economic boundaries they must overcome. When I chose not to listen to naysayers and go with my dream, I was able to help others go with theirs.

In 2009, I stepped out again into uncharted waters. After losing the rights to a contract that totaled thirty percent of my annual income, I took my first job as an employee. Since I had always worked for myself, I had to make a few social modifications, but I knew the challenge would pay off. And it did. I became the founding instructor and developer of the curriculum for Tulsa Technology Centers first Barber College, and what an extraordinary move it was! To some, it seemed as if I was abandoning my business. But in actuality, I was expanding my capacity to influence my community more profoundly.

During my tenure there, I encountered many students who had been told by their family and friends that failure would be their only option. Some heard, "You are just like your deadbeat father," or, "You're just like your deserting mother." Like myself, many were told they would not succeed because of their ethnicity, age, or past mistakes. Unfortunately, many of my students had yielded to these judgments, believing them to be true.

A large percentage of my students enrolled in my course as their last resort for a better life, but they continued to believe the lies. Many of them were former felons, high school dropouts, and former addicts. Some were just victims of their environment, not knowing they had a choice in the matter. One pupil was hooked on drugs and only lasted two months in the program. Shortly after being released from the college due to his drug use, he decided to rob a bank. My heart was broken. I know helping everyone is impossible, but it still hurts. However, after my experience with Tre' and hearing the hearts of my students during many orientations and personal development sessions, I knew I was in the right place.

The theory of "external locus of control," originated by American psychologist Julian B. Rotter, states that outside sources often influence human behavior. Studies showed that people generally respond to outside stimuli and do not exercise control. Rotter's other theory is called "internal locus of control." People that fall into this category believe they are responsible for their behavior, and therefore, take responsibility for their actions. If there is any truth to either of Rotter's theories, it's apparent that it is almost impossible for people to manage their lives if they don't first believe that their choices will affect their outcomes. Had my mother not led me to believe that my choices matter, being a victim could have possibly been my legacy. I learned to fold and declare a misdeal if I didn't like the cards life dealt to me.

> *We're not an inferior species like dogs, cats, or other life forms. Unlike animals, we greet each other with a handshake, a slight nod of the head, a hug, a kiss, or other kind gestures, right? We don't sniff each other's butts like dogs. In general, dogs will always sniff to meet and discern unless we humans train them otherwise. My point is this: **Our lives are not governed by instinct, but by our human willpower.** As we grow in confidence to make the tough choices, we gain*

the power to resist the mindset of a victim and regain controlling rights to our very souls.

Your human will to choose is key to living a good life. You must find your voice and exercise your authority in and over everything under your control. Don't allow anyone to influence you against your convictions. Stay focused and honor yourself by being the sole agent of your decisions. What you will gain is far better and worth more than anything you will lose.

I chose to forgive and love my father despite his rejection of me. I decided to DREAM ANOTHER DREAM, although others discounted my desires. If you decide to do the same, your dreams can soon become your reality too.

There are three final things I want to say about making choices. They are critical because some things can't be fixed or reversed. So, you must pay attention to the following three points.

    1) Embrace your gift of choice. Your choices are your seeds to plant into your own life to produce whatever harvest you desire. So, use this gift responsibly as every opportunity will

matter. Don't allow your bad habits, negative feelings, or other people's opinions to choose for you if the possible consequences aren't best. Be intentional with every decision. Let your past mistakes be a lesson for you; let them guide you in the right direction. Choose only what will add value to you and others.

2) Make informed decisions. *Your ignorance will not pardon you from the consequences of your wrong choices.* Be diligent in seeking wise counsel when you don't know what to do. Get advice from credible sources who have a genuine concern for your wellbeing. Because when left alone, your perspective is limited. Be humble and be open to any information that will help you make the right decisions for you and your family. When you experience good results from making wise choices, it will build your confidence in making even more right choices.

3) Keep your emotions in check. *Don't abandon what you know to be best for your life for what feels right.* Be proactive

by deferring your choices until your head is clear so you don't make decisions you may ultimately regret. Avoid pressure by making people wait for your answers so you won't surrender to their control. *You can always say, "Let me think about it: I'm not sure, I'll get back with you." But the best of all responses may be "NO." If you don't choose, others will gladly decide for you.* Your core values predetermine your choices. Therefore, be careful to keep those values, priorities, and desired outcomes in mind before making decisions.

CHAPTER NINE:
WHAT IS IN YOUR HANDS?

"A man's gift makes room for him..."

— Proverbs 18:16 (New King James Version)

People often defer their dreams because they think they must first have all their ducks in a row. In other words, they believe the timing, money, age, wardrobe, location, and skills must all be perfect before moving forward. But it's seldom that all of these are perfect at the same time. Even if it is possible, so much time will be lost waiting for it. Start right where you are with what you have.

When I was only ten years old, I was introduced to an ancient profession that transformed my life forever— barbering. Due to a misunderstanding, my family and I were evicted from an apartment complex on the west side of Tulsa, Oklahoma. As a result, my family of five moved into a small three-bedroom home with a family of three. The eviction could have been demoralizing for my family, but for me, it opened the door to discover my future career.

Darrel was a high school student who lived in the home we moved into with him and his family. Every few days, he trimmed and shaped his hair, which I found to be very intriguing. Whenever I heard the sound of his clippers buzzing, I would come running so I could watch him. While observing him, I imagined cutting my hair. Then one day, I asked if I could borrow his clippers to do so. He said, "Yes." So, I picked up the clippers and became my first client. Anyone could see I did a poor job on myself; it was nothing to brag about. But I continued to mimic what I saw, and as time passed, my skills developed. I got better and better with each trim. It wasn't long before I realized barbering indeed was my passion.

For the next several years, I was the barber for my brothers, some of my relatives, and friends. My clientele was growing by referrals. Almost every day, someone was knocking on my front door to get a haircut. I started charging five dollars per cut, which was only three dollars less than the professional prices. That inspired me to look deeper into the barbering game. I figured since preachers, teachers, moms, and even the exploiting characters from the hood like pimps, drug dealers, and gang bangers paid me as a shade tree barber, I must have been doing a pretty good job.

By the spring of my ninth-grade year—five years after the day, I picked up clippers for the first time—I heard about an apprentice program for aspiring barbers in the state of Oklahoma. At the age of fifteen, I started looking for an establishment with a master barber who would take me under their wing. I visited every barber company in my area: eight of them, to be exact. I walked, caught the city buses, and hitched rides all over my city, searching for my golden opportunity. But like most dreams worth fighting for, facing rejection was an obstacle. They all said "no" except for the last barber company I visited. I'm sure glad I didn't give up after visiting the seventh one.

Well, I thankfully accepted the position. However, I didn't expect it to be so difficult. I faced a lot of criticism. One of the older men who worked there swindled me out of some cash. Others were rude and verbally brass. Many of the clients would watch me like a hawk because of my age and inexperience. They often laughed out loud with each other over the idea of me serving them. It was almost like living the "Patrick" saga all over again. But I refused to run from the path leading to my dream.

I soon discovered I had to pay my dues and start from the bottom before working my way up. I swept up hair, took out trash, cleaned clippers and tools, and ran errands all day long. The only chore I enjoyed was picking up Pete's Famous BBQ located on 36th and Lansing, which was across the street from the barbershop. I loved hearing Ms. Pete whack that meat cleaver into a perfectly broken-in cutting board. The food was so good; I gained fifteen pounds that summer from eating that wonderfully smoked meat and sweet potato pie Ms. Pete baked herself.

All the cleaning and constant badgering got old pretty quick. I was discouraged, but I chose not to give in to the new "Patricks" of my life. So, I kept my eyes on the prize. I continued being productive, even learning how to shine shoes. Although shining shoes earned me a little money, it wasn't what I signed up to do. But it ended up being a humbling experience. For those who know about shining shoes, I can sure pop that rag and give you a spit shine.

Gratefully, I continued at that shop with an optimistic attitude because ***I knew the path to my purpose was much more profound than my performance, skills, or achievement of goals. It was about becoming my best self, not just doing my best work.*** This particular season was clearly about me becoming a servant leader. I had to learn how to lead by first serving others. It was an extraordinary season that I couldn't bypass, as it was crucial to the development of my character. It forced me to be patient and have a benevolent heart.

When I was a child, I often read parables from the Bible. The twenty-first verse of the parable found in Matthew 25 (New King James Version) says, *"Well done, thou good and faithful servant: you have been faithful over a few things, I will make you the ruler over many things."* As I appropriated what I gleaned from the story surrounding this particular verse, I trusted that serving the men's needs in the barbershop was the fastest way to my dreams. Zig Ziglar, the author of *"See You at the Top,"* and arguably the most famous salesperson in American history says, *"You can have everything in life you want if you will just help other people get what they want."* Understanding this, I continued my quest to use what was in my hands and live my purpose for that appointed time.

By the end of the summer, I finally got promoted.

Fortunately, when the opportunity presented itself, I took what was in my hands—a pair of hair clippers—and fashioned a masterpiece. I was on my way to earning enough money to fulfill many of my childhood dreams, like purchasing my first two cars at the age of sixteen. While the second car's purchase wasn't initially in the plan, I had to buy it because I totaled the first car after just two weeks of driving it. I was so upset about having to ride the school bus again. But that only lasted two weeks, at which time I bought the second one. Plus, I acquired my first home at twenty-two and opened my first retail and service establishment at twenty-three-years-old.

Today, I'm free to serve my community without the burden of trying to make ends meet. Vacations are the norm for the family. My children don't ask "if," but "when and where." I'm more than happy to take them wherever they want to go because I spent my summers as a latchkey kid who could only dream of traveling to exotic places while watching "Lifestyles of the Rich and Famous," hosted by Robin Leach back in the day.

For many of you, buying cars and taking vacations each year are easily attainable goals. But during the early years of my life, it was a mere fantasy. However, at the age of twelve, I declared I would buy a car at sixteen because my mother's car was in constant need of repair. I spoke out my desires to myself while walking to school in the cold and rain. And being unfamiliar with homeownership, I still dreamed of buying a home even though more than eighty percent of those living around me were renters. I didn't let my situation interfere with my ability to dream another dream.

I've owned and operated my own business for more than thirty years now. I travel throughout the United States to teach and train individuals from all walks of life- Working with institutions that support juvenile with behavioral and psychological challenges. I'm deeply involved in community development. I started a non-profit 501c3 organization to help kids and families with issues between the students and staff in the public school systems. I instructed countless people on how to live inspired beyond their past and present trauma.

My point? I may not be a man of great wealth, but I'm living well. My life today has been and continues to be a dream come true because I used what was in my hands. My gift used faithfully opened many doors of opportunity for me. All I have now started with what was in my hands as a teen.

Never attend the party of life empty-handed; endeavor always to have something to bring to the table— your purpose. It is required of us. Put every effort into offering your best. **And if your best isn't good enough, become better since what's in your hands is necessary and has value. You are the only one who can yield its power.** *Rest assured of this: The gift you possess will indeed make room for you. But unless it is released from your hands and distributed to the world, no one, including you, will benefit from it. Never forget that your life is the opportunity to add value to humanity. Don't make us wait too long.*

Again, just be yourself and only scale walls that are consistent with your purpose. I know you've been told, "You can be and do anything you want. Just put your mind to it." Many people with good intentions have sown this seed of false hope as a way of empowering others. But regardless of their intentions, if you believe what's not true, it will not exempt you from the consequences of failure. A single individual can't have the ability to do everything in life. Even Superman has weaknesses. So how do you find that thing that's exclusively yours? What walls are you destined to scale? What's in your hands for you to develop?

The following can guide you in discovering, developing, and becoming a servant with the God-given gifts woven in the fabric of your being as your purpose on this earth.

1) Define your gift: Usually difficult because things that come naturally for us are often overlooked as anything special. It sometimes takes others to make a big deal about them for us to realize they are gifts. However, if you don't know what your gifts are, ask others, starting with those closest to you. They will know that whatever it is you seem to do effortlessly, do better than most, and bless most with are usually your gifts. It's also often what you resort to for relaxation, do as a hobby before getting paid, or are always praised for it.

2) Develop your gifts. Even though you may have a natural gift for something, it will not hurt to find out as much as possible. Be open to more information, more instruction, and more practice. Anything, regardless of how good it is, can undergo improvement. Always be teachable because new techniques are still available to help you maintain

relevance in times that are always quickly changing. Look for other experts in the field pertinent to your gift. You already know what you know. Find out what they know.

3) Deliver your gifts through service. You will find pleasure in your contributions, but they aren't just for you. They are for as many as can benefit from them. Often your gifts will open doors to you that have nothing to do with your gifts. *It has more to do with gaining access to people with whom you wouldn't otherwise have contact.* Your gifts are gateways to more.

CHAPTER TEN:
THE BIG PICTURE

"The vision that you glorify in your mind, the ideal
that you enthrone in your heart... this you will build
your life by This you will become."

—James Allen

There is a verse in the Bible that talks about going "... from faith to faith..." (Romans 1:17 King James Version). I now understand what that means. When we conquer one giant, we feel emboldened and inspired to defeat an even bigger one. We gain strength with each victory. However, when we surrender to defeat, fear sets in like a ball and chain to keep us in the same spot. But regardless of our responses, we all have a "big picture" to consider. That picture is the blueprint of dreams. And the conclusion of our lives will either be the culmination of the best choices that lead to triumph or incorrect decisions that lead to failure. I began learning this early in life.

In 1982, I was privileged to go to a summer camp for a week. I was so excited because I didn't have many opportunities to go on a summer vacation. So, this was a big deal for me.

Summer camp consisted of delicious food, big cabins, beautiful hills, and a crystal-clear stream that seemed to have flowed right out of Eden. But what captivated me the most was the different competitions available for us kids to compete in. There was rope climbing, archery, sack races, the javelin throw, free throw contest, foot races, and swimming. The person with the most wins was crowned, "King of The Hill". My brother, Ray, won in almost every event. He was a fast runner, even faster than Patrick. As for me, there was one event in particular that I could not compete in, swimming. I didn't know how to swim at all. So, I decided to make it my goal to become a swimmer by the end of camp.

I immediately began my search for a camp counselor to teach me how to swim. Strategically, I searched for a guy that looked athletic. I found one who looked somewhat like the fictional jungle character, "Tarzan." I was sure he was a surfer or something pretty close to it. He was tall, skinny, a little animated, and had long stringy hair that he continuously flung from his eyes. I knew he was the one for the job.

After asking him to help me, he enthusiastically said, "Oh yeah, dude. I'll show you. It's easy; so easy, I bet you already know-how. You just don't know it. Trust me." His advice was phenomenal but straightforward. Move from the shallow section to the edge of the pool while staying on top of the water. Then, after showing me his swimming stroke a few times, he taught me to copy him. So, I did. Afterward, he replied, "Good job! Now go to the high dive and jump off into the deep part, but first swim several times back and forth across the pool."

With no shortage of faith, I took his word and began practicing my stroke. After making it several times across the pool, I eagerly climbed to the top of the diving board. But I was a little unprepared for what was to come. At that moment, I discovered my extreme fear of heights. My legs were shaking, and my heart began racing. So, I dropped to my knees and fearfully crawled towards the edge of the board. Though I was dripping wet from the pool water, a tsunami of sweat was pouring down my face so much I couldn't tell the difference. Yes, I was terrified but also determined to leave that camp a swimmer. After approaching the end of the board, I slowly lifted myself and rehearsed what the counselor told me.

As I stood at the diving board's edge with only water below it, there was no turning back because I had already come too far. Without any further hesitation, I jumped off the diving board into the deepest water I had ever been in. That pool was twelve feet deep. When my feet hit the water, I heard a loud clap, followed by a thump when I hit the pool's bottom. Then I pushed off the pool floor with confidence, excited to resurface to the top of the water and reach the edge. As of today, I can swim like a fish.

Most people would think the advice the counselor gave me was kind of stupid. But I chose to mix his advice with hope. The counselor painted a vivid picture of what I was to do, and it gave me a vision. And as far as I was concerned, I simply needed to believe what he said and execute it. Little did I know that my swimming experience would be an introduction to becoming a visionary for many things that were to come in my life.

My Big Picture

In 1987, I privately began a journey to change my life. I had a vision. I was thirteen years old and had reached a breaking point. I was so tired and emotionally fragmented —the idea of failure had become a stronghold. Continually vexed by a subpar image of myself, I woke up daily with the constant feeling of not measuring up. It seemed as though "Patrick" was screaming in my ears, "You'll never be good enough!" So, I prayed to God, asking Him to help me throughout my teenage years.

During that season of my life, my emotions and hormones were like attack dogs with no master to tell them to "kneel." Plus, the emotional roller coaster I was accustomed to, kept me in a constant frenzy. Sometimes, I just couldn't control my thoughts. But somehow, I knew my years as an adult would be more extended and more influential. So, I turned the tables by focusing on the years to come instead of the present. I began to imagine how I wanted my future to be while promising to make those years count.

After praying, I began to set sail towards a new place where my dreams would come true. I already knew how to dream, but I fell into a mental rut and lost sight of the big picture. I just needed to recall how good of a swimmer I had become. However, this challenge was a little deeper and more complicated than twelve feet of water. It felt as though a deep well of impossibility had come from out of nowhere. But regardless of the issue, it was still my choice to emotionally swim out of that rut or drown in defeat.

In the meantime, life continued to be an uphill battle. I was still a kid with limited resources and surrounded by a lot of nonsense. I decided the best response to this was to waste no more time with the same old folks. Instead of hanging with the crowd that did nothing for my new journey, I sat at home in a quiet spot, dreaming and devising some kind of a plan to get out of the emotional pit.

Though I was very young, all I could visualize was having a beautiful family living in a ranch-style home. In my mind's eye, I could see my kids running around playing and my life partner relaxing with her book while I'm in the backyard barbecuing while listing to a football game showing in the background. This dream was a good start to my plan, but at that time, I couldn't quite interpret its significance. But it was clear to me that this dream was about comfort and peace. I have never been materialistic. I loved family, much laughter, eating, and the greatest team sport ever: football. Although this was a very abstract visualization of my dreams, it was instrumental in keeping me optimistic. But I still needed a plan. Though I was unable to define any specific goals or objectives clearly, I was very clear about what would prevent my dream from becoming a reality: doing nothing at all.

Like Martin Luther King, Jr. said, *"You don't have to see the whole staircase, just take the first step."* And that's what I decided to do.

My first step was to avoid everything that had the potential to divert me from my big picture. At the top of the "to-be-avoided" list were drugs and alcohol. I saw firsthand how drug and alcohol abuse destroyed my father. It was apparent to me that neither would contribute to the wellbeing of my future family or myself. But despite my efforts to stay away from that lifestyle, drugs were all around me. The opportunity to sell and use drugs was presented to me by my peers as the dope dealers were often on the corner close to where we lived.

One afternoon, a peer I played football with approached me at the local corner store. He said, "What's up, Tyson? You and I can blow up (be successful). Everybody knows you. Let's slang (sell) these rocks (crack cocaine)." Along with his sister, who was a few years older and relentlessly propositioned me to have sex with her, he pressed hard to get me trapped in the dope game. But I couldn't do it. That lifestyle didn't fit into my BIG PICTURE.

It was a wild decade, but I had to stay focused. I knew for me to reach my goals, I would need money. But I had to earn it honestly. I didn't want to risk living a violent lifestyle or going to jail, which would separate me from my family. I didn't want anything to rob me of the peace of mind my mother fought so hard to attain for me. I knew if I had given in to my peers' pressure, my big picture would've ended up being nothing more than nightmare.

Self-assured, the same guy came to my house weeks later asking me again to sell crack cocaine with him. Crack cocaine was indeed the big money opportunity in the hood. And like so many others, he felt that since everyone seemed to be pushing (selling) it, why not us? But again, I said, "No." However, this time was different. As he left the house, he slipped a significant amount of crack-cocaine on the table to tempt me.

I have to admit that I thought about taking him up on the offer for just a moment. I pondered the idea of selling the drugs to make some quick money. I was tempted because we could have used the cash to get the air conditioner working again. I also thought, *Maybe I could help with a few bills or purchase a pair of new Michael Air Jordan's just that one time.* That moment offered me a choice of two paths: my current reality or the big picture of my desired future. Because my big picture was fixed in my mind and planted so deep in my heart, I chose to follow it. I had enough wisdom to know the wrong decision would not have been a one-time event. One time always turns into two, then three, then again and again. So, I chose to stay the path and flushed the drugs down the toilet.

Sadly, many of my peers and many others who pressed me to denounce my goals chose what our physical environment offered us. As a result, they are incarcerated, dependent on drugs or alcohol, or dead due to violence. Some of them continue to chase fulfillment in the wrong places, only to be denied. I wish they could have seen life through a different set of lenses. It breaks my heart when I revisit my past, knowing that some of them believed a lie. Only if they had a big picture dream.

I was fortunate to have seen an alternative path and focus my thoughts on something greater. I knew my surroundings suggested my chances of success would be slim, but my big picture was as relevant and real to me as the world around me. Our God-given abilities to imagine and dream are for these moments—to overcome overpowering odds. Hope in a promising vision allowed me to visualize alternate possibilities— to see through my darkest moments, hear over the chaos, and continue believing in myself.

Reflecting on this current season of my life, I've had to ask myself, "How did I ever get out of that funk?" Then I'm reminded of my dream. As I share my story, I often question others about what's holding them back from dreaming bigger. It pains me to see others unfulfilled because I want more for everyone.

Years ago, I declared to God that I would make a difference in people's lives, and I meant it. However, I knew wanting more for others was not enough to change their lives. That's something only they can do. And one imperative component to a life change is knowing and responding to a well-defined purpose. Undoubtedly, a clear vision is necessary to build faith for anyone's life journey.

Just like everyone else, I'm not perfect, and I do fail at times. I fail a lot. But that's why I need a plan. Though it's not easy to follow, I'm still required to submit to a vision worthy of my dreams. Its purpose is to hold me accountable when times get tough. And regrettably, over the years, I have strayed from the plan, causing much heartache and pain. But the vision remained within me to advise and remind me that my dreams wait for my cooperation. Ultimately, the goal motivates me to pursue my dreams after falling off the bandwagon vigorously.

So, how about it? Can you now see the light? Is there a big picture dream you've been waiting to live? If so, define it! Make it plain. Talk about it. Write it out so you can see it. Wake up! Visualize your desires daily until they become your internal reality. And please, don't complicate it. Your dream is simply a BIG PICTURE of your heart's desire. So, go to it every day. Declare your value and imagine living inside that big picture.

To help you stay focused on the big picture, the keys below may give you an advantage as they did for me. There will be obstacles. But staying committed to a defined written plan will provide you with a better chance of succeeding.

1) **Attitude:** Be positive, Smile, and Believe you will achieve your desires.

2) **Vision:** Write what you desire several times a day, every day until you understand it clearly.

3) **Information:** Educate yourself about what you want. For one hour daily, develop your skills, collect data, and develop the relationships you need to achieve your goals.

4) **Plan:** Develop a strategy. Create simple "1-2-3" steps arranged in a logical order that will cover YOUR MISSION, YOUR GOALS, and YOUR OBJECTIVES.

5) **Guidance:** Discuss your plans with three mentors or leaders weekly. No one does it alone.

6) **Words:** SPEAK YOUR DESIRES DAILY and imagine living the life you want UNTIL YOUR DREAM BECOMES YOUR INTERNAL REALITY. Set your alarm on your phone to alert you every few hours to

speak positive things pertinent to your desires until you develop confidence that comes from speaking and hearing it repeatedly.

7) **Take Action:** Growth does not happen in your past or your future. It occurs at the moment you are experiencing right now.

Be intentional. Apply these steps and watch your desires come to life. You will have fewer distractions, and your mind will become less cluttered. Now, go live the DREAM!

TYSON D. THOMPSON

CHAPTER ELEVEN: BECOME THE DREAM

"You must conform to your desires while they are still inside of you before they can manifest outwardly. "—Tyson D. Thompson

There is a difference between a "dream" and a "fleeting fantasy." Dreams of substance will stay with you and manage to take over your head and your heart. Fantasies are often replaced relatively quickly with new fantasies because they are only meaningful in your head. But no dream will come to pass until you first let the dream do preliminary work in you. *You must conform to your desires while they are still inside of you before they can manifest outwardly.* Let me explain.

By August 1987, after spending the summer meditating on my big picture, nothing had tangibly changed from what I could see. I still had the same old sneakers, two pairs of jeans, a flattened mattress with holes exposing the broken box spring, and my black and white thirteen-inch TV. When I looked in the mirror, those same big ears and pointed eyebrows people loved making fun of were bigger and pointier than ever. And yes, I was still short and bow-legged—5'3" tall to be exact. Though I hadn't grown one inch that summer, I knew I was a giant deep down in my spirit. Boiling over in my heart was a fountain of confidence, and a pool filled with optimism was beginning to overflow. Without a doubt, this was not just an emotional experience; I knew I had become a different person. And I have to admit; it had to be a God thing.

> *This inward transformation all began with me speaking words of affirmation to myself. Those words soon became a part of my belief system. Eventually, it became sustainable once it entered my heart. Daily, I spoke, read, and meditated on the lessons I learned over the years. Miraculously, my child-like faith revived.*

Once the 1987–1988 school year had begun, I knew what had transpired. Consequently, many others did too. Some of my classmates asked me, "What's up with you, Tyson? You're different." I did not answer and just went about my business. Without anyone's approval, I peacefully began my journey towards my dreams. I learned how to move to the beat of my own drum. Remarkably, others began to move with me. The rhythm of my life was becoming infectious. The change was mind-boggling.

That year, I was elected president of the Student Council, and president of the school's Red Cross organization. For some reason, my teacher, Earlene Gathright, encouraged me to run for those positions. I didn't think I had a chance, but she did. In previous years, I would have rejected the idea, but that year was different. Still a little doubtful of myself, I chose to run for vice president instead of president. But because of a student's conduct, she was disqualified from the presidential position, so I ran for it and won.

During the previous school year, I tried out for the basketball team. I made the team, but was a horrible player, scoring a total of only six points the entire season. And that was all in one game. However, after that disastrous year of basketball, I dreamed another dream; I tried football. Surprisingly, I became a captain on the team and was one of the best players that year.

As my teammates and I huddled around our coaches after a disappointing loss in the playoffs', one of the coaches said, "If everyone had played like Tyson, we would have won!" Even a coach from the neighboring high school referred to me as "The Leg Cutter" because of my ability to cut down opposing running backs for significant losses. What a revolutionary experience it was. It seemed as if everything I touched turned to gold.

I gained much favor with the staff, teachers, and the students of my school, including the principal. When special events were available for student participation, I was the first person the teachers asked. There were a few girls that began liking me also. I traveled to leadership camps and gatherings in other cities designed to help students excel. I was exposed to people, places, and experiences I had only imagined. And somehow, my grades were even good; so good, I was in the gifted and advanced classes. And my test scores were so high that I was accepted into the city's most prestigious high school, Booker T. Washington. Also, one of the top-ranked schools in the nation.

I was amazed because this kind of stuff never happened to me before. And fortunately, I took advantage of every one of those opportunities. I began focusing on improving my social skills by embracing other cultures. I also used my influence for social change in my school by standing up to the bullies that once terrorized me and discouraging them from doing the same to other students. In other words, I had discovered my inner voice. I no longer made excuses for who I was. I was proud to be a little Black boy who lived in the hood. I wasn't concerned about my clothes, shoes, or any other objects of vanity. I stood by my convictions even though I was called a "sellout" and "soft." I chose to appreciate all aspects of who I was.

At that point in my development, I knew I had come too far to give up. I was on a roll; nothing and no one could stop me from living well—no one. I'm so grateful to have arrived at that understanding because little did I know, my life would be a wreck one day. And that perspective would be the saving grace to put it back together again.

Becoming the dream is a process that you can start right away by implementing the following:

1) **Believe.** Faith in your dream increases as you speak words of affirmation to yourself—not just once or twice—but all the time. Create a lifestyle of speaking, listing, and

sharing. Make sure that your words are associated with core values that have merit. With time, those values will become a part of your belief system. What you say will become sustainable once it enters your heart.

2) **Act like your dream is real.** Part of becoming what you believe is to act as if it's already true. Your desire should be evident in your speech, your posture, and your attitude. It's not faking; it's training. Practice until your dream becomes your eternal and physical reality.

3) **Include others.** Understand that no one becomes successful alone. You will need help. Involve those who are interested in your success. Be open to both their encouragement and constructive criticism. Allow them to hold you accountable to be consistent with your plans. We all need someone to remind us of who we are and why we are pursuing particular desires.

CHAPTER TWELVE: DREAM ANOTHER DREAM

"And he dreamed yet another dream,
and told it his brethren, and said, Behold, I have
dreamed a dream more…"

—Genesis 37:9 (King James Version)

The Death of My Dream

In 2015, one of my most desired dreams failed; my marriage of twenty-two years had come to an end. It was such a disappointment because I was driven to get married after witnessing the failure of my parent's relationship. I thought I could right the wrongs that were done to my mother by recreating a successful marriage of my own. I chose to respect, love, and provide for my family. I handled my relationship in a way that was opposite of the way my father conducted himself with my mother. But despite my efforts, that dream crumbled. My marriage slowly seeped through my fingers like powdery white sand, which caused me to become frantic. My grip was not strong enough to hold on to what was left of the twenty-five-year relationship. The bond we had somehow vanished as if it had never existed.

Though the divorce was in full motion, I held on as long as I could. I was a bit obsessed. During our first meeting with an attorney, I attempted to stop the process, but there was no giving in—the marriage was unsalvageable. Regardless of what I said, the divorce papers were processed. As the attorney spoke, I broke down in tears. I couldn't believe what I was hearing. I thought to myself; this was not supposed to be a part of my ***BIG PICTURE DREAM***. I was so devastated I couldn't compose myself. I hurried out of the law office to collapse in the front seat of my car weeping for what I thought was my life.

I had given up on myself. It was undeniably the most demoralizing ordeal of my life. After making what seemed to be an unforgivable mistake, I drifted to a dark place of depression. Life as I knew it was over. Fortunately, I didn't want to end my life, but I no longer wanted to share it. I was ashamed, embarrassed, and grieving all at once.

At the age of forty-two, I had shut down. For months, I would sit up all night as guilt ate away at my confidence. I felt worthless. I woke up daily to the most tormenting emotions, riddled with feelings of being a traitor and a failure. What seemed like a hellish nightmare was my reality because I was wide awake, experiencing every freaking moment of the pain.

My reason for getting married may not have been the best. Nonetheless, I was committed to the idea when the opportunity presented itself. I have since realized my identity was wrapped up in the relationship so much that I had unknowingly imprisoned myself. Consequently, I was emotionally shackled to my sorrow with no way of escape. Furthermore, I bore all the blame by taking responsibility for everything wrong in the relationship as if I was liable for everyone's happiness. With that in mind, I was full of myself. By no means I was responsible for everything wrong. If that's the case, I would have been responsible for everything right as well. And that defiantly wasn't true. It takes two to tango. Anyway, my marriage had become my everything; it was my idol.

My mornings were tough. At 5:45 a. m. , every Monday, Wednesday, and Friday, after pulling up to the gym to play ball and lift weights, I would just sit in my car, contemplating whether to go in or not. When I opened the car door, my legs felt as heavy as the weights I was about to lift. I dreaded the idea of facing anyone. Even though only a few people knew my story, it felt like the world was watching and discussing my every move on social media. I just knew the guys I played basketball with were judging me.

I've always been positive and optimistic about my future, and rarely worried about anything. Though, like everyone else, I struggled in a few areas. But I maintained a supernatural belief that somehow things would always get better and work out in my favor. But during that time, I wasn't feeling that way at all. Guilt had stripped me of my faith. It seemed as if the God my mother taught me about was not speaking to me anymore. My shameful behavior had separated me from what I knew to be true. I couldn't hear a word. I felt all alone and was uncertain of what the outcome of my life would be. But there was also a more pressing concern: my children.

The divorce affected my children worse than I could have ever imagined. They were completely innocent in the matter, yet it impacted their lives just as it did mine. I barely knew how to respond when my oldest daughter cried out in an angry voice to me with her face drenched in tears: "Daddy! Why did you allow this to happen?" Not knowing what else to say at that moment, I responded with, "I can't answer you fully now, but I'm sorry."

How could I have been so self-centered? A good friend, who was also my mentor, forewarned me because he had a very similar encounter with his daughter. He warned me to get my affairs in order before I suffer the same consequence. But I ignored his wisdom. That day, I wept like a baby seeing how my daughter was emotionally distraught because of me. My youngest daughter also cried when she first heard the news about her mother and me. But her crying soon turned into penetrating screams of agony as she discovered her parents were breaking up. As for my only son, he couldn't even look me in the eyes without displaying his anger and disappointment towards me. After confessing my faults to him, in a personal narrative, he wrote:

> *"My crystal-clear image of my father began to crack and erode into a stained mess. The anger and pure rage that I felt toward him at the moment for causing my family such pain was so strong that I felt like I was going to explode."*

Those moments with my children caused me to become even more anxious. My guilt was choking the life out of me. My mind was utterly chaotic. For weeks, I was hopeless in my attempts to conceal my shame. One day while working, my business partner asked if I was okay. I told him that I was good, but he saw right through me, knowing I had lied. But I felt all was lost. All I had was a front-row seat as I watched what appeared to be a cinematic screenplay of a family's demise—me being the villain.

As my family was unraveling right before me, I thought, My God, my God, what happened to my dream? Though weeping and sorrowful crying had become the echoing sound throughout my once loving home, I sat waiting for someone to yell, "Cut!" and put an end to the horror movie I was watching. It was almost unbearable.

I was reckless in my thinking. Considering my conduct, it was inevitable that this day was coming. I saw it but refused to accept it. And when that day arrived, I was awakened to the reality I had been a fool—full of pride—not willing to deal with my true feelings. Fearful of confronting pertinent issues over the years eventually came back to haunt me. Ultimately, I had emotionally shut out my family and opened the door that lead to its end.

I Dreamed A New Dream

In December of 2015, after having a disturbing discussion about my children's custody, I laid down on the sofa in my family room. My eyes were swollen with tears as I tried to hold on to what little faith I had left—it wasn't much. However, I still needed to know what to do next. Stressed and heavy-hearted, my mind simply could not pull together a plan. All I knew was my dream had died, and my children were suffering.

Then suddenly, I heard a still, small voice say to me, "Get up!" It was as if it was spoken from deep within my heart: "Get up!" When I lifted my head and wiped the tears from my face, I heard this:

> Get up. Go and do what you know. You have a plan and a purpose still. Get up! Although your mistakes have great consequences, your purpose is greater. Your life exists for more than just you and your family. Don't allow yourself to be ruined over one relationship. Yes, mistakes were made, but you are not a mistake. Remember your initial dream. Don't forget what that entails. Get up! Read the manuscript

that's in your heart. It will reveal to you precisely
what to do.

I hesitated for a moment. Because for some time, the inner guidance I was accustomed to following was silent. But with tears streaming down my face, I grabbed my Mac Book Pro, typed in my password, and began to read. As I recited the words from my manuscript, ***"... my value cannot be taken,"*** I began to feel comforted. I was astonished that the answers I needed had been lying dormant within me the entire time!

I had been masking my true beliefs for years and had lost my inner voice again. Thankfully, the still small voice was right. It was the same voice of reasoning that encouraged me to dream another dream when I was a five-year-old boy. It was the voice that inspired a change in my life when I was thirteen years old—the same persuading voice that said to me, "You have a dream. Don't sell those drugs." It was the same voice that prepared me at fifteen years old to recognize my moment and take advantage of what I had in my hands. The same power that reminds me daily that life is a gift, and it must be shared.

Although the dream of a "perfect marriage" ended, the essence of my dream was still alive and well. I had come to realize that a happy marriage was not my dream in the first place. My marriage was to be a relationship purposed to assist me through life and deliver value to my family and the world. My initial dream is and has always been about people and their meaning.

As for my purpose, it was apparent to me. I was still a father to my children and a friend to their mother. My position as a son to my mother hadn't changed either. My siblings never stopped calling me, "Bro." And seeing how my responsibilities as a servant-leader at my company had not lost its value—I was still in the game.

> *To sum it up, the world didn't stop spinning on its axis because of me. Life continued whether I was going to be a part of it or not. And people were just as valuable despite my stupidity.* ***Flaws and all, what I had to offer was still tremendously valuable.*** *So, I humbled myself and respected the fact that my family needed me more than ever. I stopped crying and got busy, for my pain did not pardon me from my obligations. That part deserves repeating:* ***MY PAIN DID NOT PARDON ME FROM MY OBLIGATIONS.***

I was still obligated to fulfill my role as a loving father and friend. I was responsible for helping my family navigate through this tough period. Therefore, I eagerly resumed my role as the "leader" I had committed to be. I remembered that Agape love requires something of me regardless of my unhappiness, and that is to LOVE FIRST. Then I was able to DREAM ANOTHER DREAM.

After spending some time processing my new dream, I sat my children down, to share how we were going to handle the trauma. This is what I said to them:

> As of today, our lives will be better than ever. Why? Because you and I will choose to make it so. I know this is a tough time for you all, but you will get through this. And I will not allow you to use this as an opportunity to make excuses for dysfunctional behavior. I know this is hard, but your identity and self-worth are not in your mother and me being together. **Your existence is not predicated upon a marriage**. You could have been born whether your mother and I were married or not. Like me and millions of other families who suffered through divorce, you can make it, and you will. We have a choice. Now

let's choose to enjoy the rest of our lives together.
Daddy loves you."

I must confess, being engaged at the young age of seventeen and getting married at the age of nineteen came with its own set of challenges. And quite frankly, I wasn't prepared. Heck! I would argue that most adults aren't ready for marriage, let alone teenagers. Nevertheless, that was no excuse for me to bail on my family. I was forty-two at that time and was determined to see this new dream through. Like Grant Cardone says in his book, 10X Rule: "You can never lose the ability to come up with new dreams." I did just that. ***I got gritty about keeping my family together. Although this was not how I envisioned it, I insisted that the new dream will prevail.***

TYSON D. THOMPSON

CONCLUSION

L ife can be good. Life can also be a living hell. But how you choose to view it and how you choose to live is up to you. You may experience unavoidable turmoil that's the result of others' choices. You can either be defined by it or let it redefine your character by choosing to love unconditionally and value yourself and others despite it. The choice is yours.

After living on this earth for forty-six years now, it is still my endeavor to live a better life and strive for excellence. However, I'm not perfect. I've failed to nurture relationships. I've mismanaged funds. I've laughed at others when it wasn't polite. And, at times, I've even neglected my children. Though I would need all of my 256-gigabyte hard drive on my iPhone to contain my list of failures, my value cannot be diminished. I'm at a place where I can vow never to let another dream die. Life has taught me how to do that. I'm adhering to what Langston Hughes once said: "Hold fast to dreams. For if dreams die, life is a broken-winged bird that cannot fly." I'm determined never to be broken again; I will value myself and hold fast to my dreams. Will you join me?

Let everything that challenges you become your opportunity to learn how to overcome and grow into the person you indeed are. As you may have already heard, "You are not what you go through." So just accept your human experiences as necessary parts of your human development. How you choose to respond to a painful past or current opposition will determine your mindset for future endeavors. Achieving your goal of having a good life without simultaneously developing your character defeats the purpose.

Success is not just about your personal goals, achievements, or vain desires. It's about your development as a human being, which is, by far, your most significant accomplishment as it affects everything in your life, including the people in your sphere of influence. It's about taking responsibility for how you respond to life instead of making others responsible for your responses. It's about making the most of what you already have, right where you are, right now. It's about managing your emotions, understanding that how you feel doesn't change your value. It's about realizing that your gifts, talents, and acquired skills are for you to share with the world.

You've been graced with the gift of life, and it demands of you to know, accept, and fulfill your purpose. Even when people you love repeatedly let you down. Others' opinions of you don›t validate your self-worth. Plus, your view of yourself must not be tainted by your past mistakes. Mistakes are a part of life, but you must keep them in perspective, learn from them, and grow beyond them. *USE ALL THAT YOU ARE TO ADD MORE VALUE TO THIS WORLD'S GREATEST TREASURE: PEOPLE.*

Let me warn you as well as encourage you. Holding fast to your DREAM is a lifelong ambition that you must defend almost daily. You must guard yourself against petty and irrelevant matters to maintain the enthusiasm necessary to propel you upward. Know that you will need to be open to new relationships that are relative to your journey. They may not be direct participants in your dream, but they may help shape your character and build your confidence along the way.

C. S. Lewis said it best: *"You are never too old to set another" goal or to dream a new dream."* I absolutely agree with *Lewis.* So please, NO EXCUSES! Don't wait for favorable conditions or people to cosign on your dream as neither may never happen. Don't wait for acceptance and love, or for every "Patrick" to disappear.

Remember, your self-imposed limitations can only bound you. So, go ahead, DREAM ANOTHER DREAM!

CITATIONS

"There is no Frigate like a book." — Emily Dickinson
The Poems of Emily Dickinson Edited by R. W. Franklin
(Harvard University Press, 1999)

"Try not to become a man of success, but rather try to
become a man of value."[1]

"Every great dream begins with a dreamer. Always
remember, you have within you the strength, the
patience, and the passion to reach for the stars to change
the world." — Harriet Tubman[2]

"What do you do when one dream fails? Dream another
dream." — Peter Daniels[3]

"Better a diamond with a flaw than a pebble without."
— Confucius[4]

"A man is literally what he thinks, his character being the

---

[1]Quote by Albert Einstein recorded by journalist William
Miller, printed in Life Magazine in 1955.
[2]www.goodreads.com › quotes
[3]How to Reach Your Life Goals: Keys to Help You Fulfill
Your Dreams, Published January 1st 1985 by The House of
Tabor
[4]Confucius (551–479 BC) was a Chinese teacher, editor,
politician, and philosopher of the Spring and Autumn
period of Chinese history.

complete sum of all his thoughts." —James Allen[5]

...Stephen Curry, the superstar point guard of the NBA.[6]

Albert Einstein shared the same idea as he stated: "Great spirits have always encountered violent opposition from mediocre minds."[7]

"Think and Grow Rich" — Napoleon Hill says this:

You have absolute control over but one thing, and that is your thoughts. This is the most significant and inspiring of all facts known to man! It reflects man's divine nature. This divine prerogative is the sole means by which you may control your own destiny. If you fail to control your own mind, you may be sure you will control nothing else. If you must be careless with your possessions, let it be in connection with material things. Your mind is your spiritual estate! Protect and use it with the care to which divine royalty is entitled. You were given a willpower for this purpose.[8]

---

[5]*As a Man Thinketh* Published December 28th 2006 by TarcherPerigee (first published 1902 by James Allen)
[6]*FOOTNOTES Wardell Stephen Curry II*, American professional basketball player for the Golden State Warriors with the NBA. Career period 2009-present. https://www.britannica.com/biography/Stephen-Curry

[7]Quoted in a symposium, 1941. (1879–1955)
[8]FOOTNOTES Napoleon Hill, published by The Ralston Society in 1937

"Life is a matter of choices, and every choice you make makes you."—John C. Maxwell[9] (2011).

Lloyd E. Rader Treatment Center in Sand Springs, Oklahoma. Lloyd E. Rader[10]

Dr. Bob Harrison, also known as "Dr. Increase". He was responsible for bailing out a major Chrysler dealership in California during the 1970's gas crisis.[11]

In 1921, there was a horrible massacre in Tulsa, Oklahoma that destroyed an area called "Black Wall Street."[12]

For example, slavery in America was followed by Jim Crow laws which perpetuated the same system of slavery through politics, law enforcement, corporations, school systems, and other institutions. This approach was intended to be more subtle than the physical chains of slavery. [13]

---

[9]*Beyond Talent: Become Someone Who Gets Extraordinary Results*, John C. Maxwell (2011). p.10, Thomas Nelson Inc
[10]*L.E. Rader Center* closed permanently in September 2011 ...www.tulsaworld.com › news › local › government-and-politics. Posted April 2011
[11]https://churchoftheword.com/speakers/bob-harrison/
[12]*The Burning: Massacre, Destruction, and the Tulsa Race Riot of 1921* by Tim Madigan.
[13]The roots of Jim Crow laws began as early as 1865, immediately following the ratification of the 13th Amendment which abolished slavery in the United States.

...Tulsa Tech's first Barber College[14]

The theory of "external locus of control," originated by American psychologist Julian B. Rotter, states that human behaviour is often influenced by outside sources. Studies showed that people generally respond to outside stimuli and do not exercise control.[15]

Rotter's other theory is called "internal locus of control." People that fall into this category believe they are responsible for their behaviour, and therefore, take responsibility for their actions.[16]

Pete's Famous BBQ located on 36th and Lansing[17]

Zig Ziglar, the author of "See You at The Top," and arguably the most famous sales person in American history says, "You can get everything in life you want if you will just help enough other people get what they want."[18]

---

[14] *Tulsa Tech* was established in Tulsa, Oklahoma in 1965 www. https://tulsatech.edu/

[15] Krampen, G. (2005). Psychology of Control and Personality: Julian B. Rotter and Beyond.

[16] Krampen, G. (2005). Psychology of Control and Personality: Julian B. Rotter and Beyond.

[17] *Pete's Famous BBQ* opened in 1968 and closed in 2001. www.tulsapeople.com › table-talk › the-business-of-barbecue

[18] *See You at the Top* by Zig Ziglar Arcadia Publishing SC, 2000 (revised)

"Lifestyles of the Rich and Famous" hosted by Robin Leach[19]

"The vision that you glorify in your mind, the ideal that you enthrone in your heart… this you will build your life by. This you will become."—James Allen[20]

fictional jungle character, "Tarzan."[21]

Like Martin Luther King, Jr. said, "You don't have to see the whole staircase, just take the first step."[22]

…the city's most prestigious high school, Booker T. Washington.[23]

Like Grant Cardone says in his book, 10X Rule: "You can

[19]*Lifestyles of the Rich and Famous with Robin Leach* first on television from 1984 to 1985. Robin Leach died on August 24, 2018. https://www.imdb.com/title/tt0086750/?ref_=ttpl_pl_tt

[20]"James Lane Allen Quotes." BrainyQuote.com. BrainyMedia Inc, 2020. 13 March 2020. https://www.brainyquote.com/quotes/james_lane_allen_194683

[21]Tarzan The Ape Man is a fictional character originated April 3, 1932. https://www.imdb.com/title/tt0023551/

[22]Martin Luther King, Jr. gave a speech on September 12, 1962, at the Park-Sheraton Hotel in New York City.

[23]Booker T. Washington, a high school established in Tulsa, Oklahoma in 1913. Named after the African-American education pioneer Booker T. Washington.

never lose the ability to come up with new dreams."[24]

What Langston Hughes once said: "Hold fast to dreams. For if dreams die, life is a broken-winged bird that cannot fly."[25]

C.S. Lewis said it best: "You are never too old to set another goal or to dream a new dream."[26]

---

[24] *The 10X Rule*- Grant Cardone; Wiley; 1 edition (April 26, 2011)
[25] *The Collected Poems of Langston Hughes* published by Alfred A. Knopf/Vintage. Copyright © 1994 by the Estate of Langston Hughes.
[26] C.S. Lewis (1898-1963) Writer, Theologian, Scholar

ABOUT THE AUTHOR
TYSON D. THOMPSON

Tyson D. Thompson is a consummate educator and business professional. Best known for his irresistible passion for inspiring people.

He has spent more than 30 years as an instructor, master barber, mentor, and life coach, equipping individuals and organizations to overcome hardship and conquer social disparities— turning his love for educating others into practical seminars, keynote addresses, and literature.

Alongside his wife, son, and three daughters, he's inspired to write and teach us how to continue Dreaming New Dreams and add value to the world.

TYSON D. THOMPSON

Made in USA - Kendallville, IN
1205100_9781736020401
12.03.2020 1558